Career Turbulence

Ancient Lessons for Survival in the Modern Workplace

Robert C. Lerner

First Edition

Oshawa, Ontario

Career Turbulence:
Ancient Lessons for Survival in the Modern Workplace
by Robert C. Lerner

Managing Editor:	Kevin Aguanno
Typesetting:	Carolyn Prior, Kevin Aguanno
Cover Design:	Robert Lerner/Charles Sin
eBook Conversion:	Carolyn Prior

Published by:
Multi-Media Publications Inc.
Box 58043, Rosslynn RPO, Oshawa, ON, Canada, L1J 8L6.
http://www.mmpubs.com/

All rights reserved. No part of this book may be reproduced or transmitted in any form or by any means, electronic or mechanical, including photocopying, recording or by any information storage and retrieval system, without written permission from the publisher, except for the inclusion of brief quotations in a review.

The contents of this book are presented for educational and discussion purposes only. The publisher and author make no warranties of whether they are fit for any particular use.

Copyright © 2014 by Multi-Media Publications Inc.

Paperback	ISBN-13: 9781554891702
eBook	ISBN-13: 9781554891719

Published in Canada. Printed simultaneously in Canada, the United States of America, Australia, and the United Kingdom.

CIP data available from the publisher.

Table of Contents

Foreword..9

Introduction...13

The Early Life of Atticus....................35

    Lesson 1: Self-promotion is no Vice..........43
    Lesson 2: Cultivate the Powerful.............45
    Lesson 3: Get the hell out of Dodge..........49
    Lesson 4: Cash is King...........................52
    Lesson 5: Firmness is not Synonymous with Abrasiveness................56
    Lesson 6: Do not Dismiss the Value of an Occasional Overstatement.................59
    Lesson 7: Obsess about Timing................61

A Banker in Athens...........................67

    Lesson 8: Consider Neutrality as an Option in a Political Conflict 74
    Lesson 9: It's Who you Know that Makes the Difference................................78
    Lesson 10: Self-Preservation Trumps Trust...83
    Lesson 11: Do not Underestimate the Power of Tenacity.............................87

Career Turbulence

Wealth Preservation in Rome..........91

Lesson 12: Skepticism is a Virtue............96
Lesson 13: Keep your Passions in Check 101
Lesson 14: The Deferral of Difficult Decisions Courts Disaster......................108
Lesson 15: Adapt as Circumstances Demand..112

The Ides of March and Its Aftermath..119

Lesson 16: Keep your Ears Open............126
Lesson 17: Do not Persist in Error.........130
Lesson 18: In a Crisis it is Best to Hedge your Bets.....................................137

The End Game for Cicero and Atticus..145

Lesson 19: Politics is More Marathon than Sprint.............................149
Lesson 20: The Ends Justifies the Means..153

Atticus and his Legacy.....................157

Appendices

    A: Additional Information on Nepos...171

    B: Nepos and Cicero..................173

    C: Cicero's Self-Censorship...................177

    D: Atticus' Lifestyle..................179

    E: End Notes..............................181

    F: Bibliography.........................201

Index of Names....................209

About the Author............................221

Acknowledgements

Writing a business book about Cicero's banker, Atticus, had been a goal of mine for a number of years, but I could never find the appropriate context. However, as my daughters worked to find their way in a post-2008 economy, I realized that now was the appropriate time to provide a study of the lessons to be learned from a man like Atticus. Atticus lived in extremely difficult times, and I am indebted to Professor Jacqueline Carlon, whose guidance on this complex period of Roman history was invaluable. In the process of creating this work I asked numerous friends for their insights into the mind of a businessman such as Atticus. In particular, the feedback of Gerry Kappus, Lynn Wegner and Dr. Glen Wegner was essential to the framing of this work. I would also like to express my gratitude to Dr. Mark Zupan for his recommendations for improving the structure of the text and commentary. I also want to thank Mark Kozak-Holland for his commitment to the development of this project and Chris Stanvick

Career Turbulence

for her meticulous review of the manuscript, but of course any errors or misinterpretation of the sources, whether ancient or modern, are solely my responsibility. Last, but certainly not least, I am indebted to my wife for her infinite patience with the time I consumed in completing this project.

Foreword

Writing a foreword to a book is an honor usually given to a well-known individual who might assist in the promotion of the book. In this instance, however, I know Bob asked me to fulfill this task for a different reason. Bob solicited my efforts specifically because I experienced the loss of a job and struggled to regain my status (which now includes a 3000-mile weekly round trip commute from Boston to my Tampa office). For almost a quarter of a century, as a Human Resources professional in both the public and private sector, and like millions around the globe, I too had withstood, "the blows" of the marketplace. As an adopted son of an old mill town in Massachusetts, where jobs were lost to foreign competition, and where a computer giant was born and flourished, (Wang Laboratories) creating thousands of local, (and global) jobs and then collapsed into bankruptcy leading to careers again being destroyed, I thought I had experienced it all. But unlike Cicero's banker Atticus, I failed to survive one last crisis with the result that job preservation was replaced with job solicitation.

Career Turbulence

This is not a traditional handbook to business success. This unique and thoughtful approach of bringing ancient Rome back to life and allowing the reader to connect the ages is exceptional. It can either be a handbook to laying the ground work for an up and coming career or as in my case a reflective review of how I made it without even knowing that I was following the advice and career of Atticus. The handbook has many different themes and lessons that will resonate with all who choose a business or political career path. Many of the lessons presented here are actually life lessons, many of which we should have all learned from our parents or those individuals who guided us during our youth. Strongly cultivated individual relationships with measured loyalty, (but always with an eye towards self-preservation) and of course competence were key elements to Atticus' success. Those are the basics to business success today; some may call it the "art of politics".

This past summer, after reading an early draft of this book, I spent two weeks exploring Rome and Pompeii. The ancient ruins are amazing but at the end of each day my thoughts were not on the architecture but on the political and business infrastructure of those ancient cities; the world of Caesar, Cicero and of course Atticus. The players in that ancient drama have modern day counterparts making modern day business and political decisions. During those reflective moments overlooking the ruins of the Roman Forum from the rooftop of the Forum Hotel, I was both amazed at how different the world has become as well as how similar it remains. This work is a novel and scholarly approach to bridging the ages by illustrating that basic personal

Foreword

business strategies were not developed in the age of the Internet or even during the industrial revolution. The strategies are as old as Rome itself, battle worn and tested by the ages.

As an HR executive, setting aside my personal career, I have watched and counseled business professionals navigating through individual careers during amazing periods of unprecedented growth and business stability as well as turbulent times when sales are plummeting, margins depressed and the lack of profits causing large reductions in force. I have seen the "Rock Star" high potential recruit burn out quickly due to not understanding the political landscape of an organization. I have also been witness to the young executive that was competent, who learned all aspects of the business, who aligned himself with key leaders of the organization and who survived a devastating bankruptcy period. This handbook is actually a blueprint designed to assist those willing to learn from history the secrets to positioning for success. It is not uncommon for business leaders like Bob Lerner (for whom I spent many years working as his HR executive) upon leaving the "arena" to write about their career, their strategies, their successes and once in a great while their failures. This is not a retrospective look at a senior executive's career - it is a senior executive providing historical path for individual success utilizing a path as old as the ancient Appian Way.

Norm Lombardi,
Senior Vice President, Human Resources
Valet Waste, Inc. Tampa, FL

Career Turbulence

CHAPTER 1

Introduction

Generating personal financial security, whether by means of employment in a small to medium sized company, or a career in a large corporation, is difficult even on "good days" and seemingly impossible during turbulent times. Most often your financial wellbeing is dependent on employment, and so the loss of a job often can result in the complete destruction of your personal wealth. In the toughest of economic times, remaining employed is even more critical because once lost, a well-paid job may be impossible to replace. This proximity to financial disaster became glaringly obvious to millions of families as a result of the devastating recession that began in 2007/2008.

The cascading effects of that severe economic downturn created crushing financial pressure on businesses with the result that in 2010 there were over 1 million company failures in the U.S. alone.[1] With businesses failing at such a significant rate and surviving businesses curtailing hiring as well as laying off workers to reduce expenditures, U.S.

Career Turbulence

unemployment rates quickly escalated, reaching double digits (see Figure 1.1). Additionally U.S. mortgage delinquencies skyrocketed (see Figure 1.2) and housing foreclosures topped a staggering 3.8 million homes in 2010.[2]

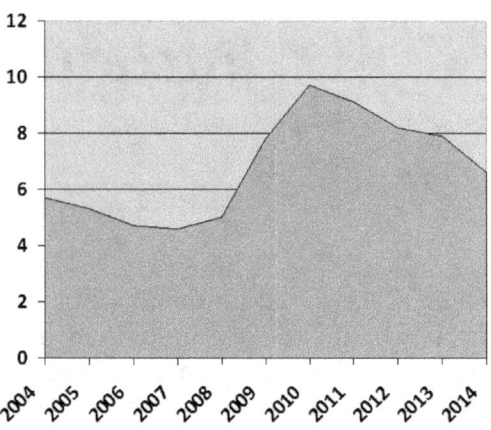

Figure 1.1: This chart is a graph of the U.S. unemployment rate from 1/1/02 to 1/1/13. Unemployment peaked in the fall of 2009 at just over 10% and has declined from that high with agonizingly slow progress. (Source: U.S. Dept. of Labor, Bureau of Labor Statistics)

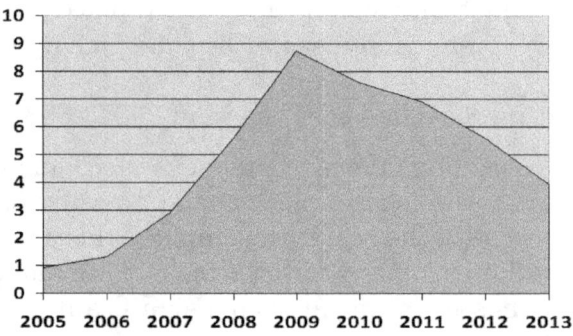

Figure 1.2: This chart shows the skyrocketing growth in mortgage delinquencies from 2005-2012. (Source: FRBNY Consumer Credit Panel/Equifax).

1 - Introduction

Clearly, in this type of economic free-fall, personal wealth preservation simply meant job preservation. Unfortunately the impact of this macroeconomic crisis that has reverberated through the global economy for years now has not fully dissipated and unemployment still languishes at painfully elevated levels.

The Impact of Turbulence on Career Management Strategies

From an individual's perspective the long-lasting turbulence engendered by a financial crisis that began in 2007/2008 can cripple the normal decision-making processes that employees, managers, and executives typically utilize in their career planning. Therefore the preservation of your employment in such times requires a dramatically different approach than that typically adopted when you are competing in a marketplace that is much more quiescent. A key reason for this added complexity is that there is such uncertainty in the marketplace that rational analysis becomes impaired – there is often just not sufficient clarity of data to choose a safe harbor in which to weather the storm, let alone to find the best means for advancement.
In such times a different set of rules needs to be followed - rules far more Darwinian than in normal economic times. Expedience and self-interest must emerge as critical components of your job survival strategy when the alternative is personal economic destruction.

The Occurrence of Market Turbulence

Hopefully such turbulent periods occur with relative infrequency in each generation (although if you are enduring one, frequency is irrelevant). The macroeconomic cycles of expansion followed by contraction can be the result of a broad spectrum of economic disturbances ranging from inflationary booms to failed governmental monetary policies to war. We are not here, however, to debate the underlying causes of such economic distress. Instead the intent of this work is to recognize that since these periods of economic dislocation have occurred with disappointing frequency and have been of frustratingly long duration, a set of job preservation lessons may help ensure that the reader is better prepared to deal with both the remaining years of the current crisis and the onslaught of the next.

This periodicity of economic distress also means that economic crises, sometimes of much greater intensity than that currently being endured, have occurred in the past and therefore there is a unique opportunity for us to study and learn from those who have successfully navigated the turbulent times that they were forced to endure. Insights gained from studying even a single successful survival story of the past can be incorporated into your current career preservation strategy. Any knowledge gained is useful in a crisis since typically when one is in survival mode there is not much opportunity to learn from mistakes, and failure is simply not an option.

1 - Introduction

Author's Familiarity with Managing in Turbulent Times

Having endured a large corporate bankruptcy (Wang Laboratories in 1992), corporate takeovers (both as an acquirer and the acquired), divestitures, the economic aftermath of 9/11, the anthrax scare of '02 and early stages of the great recession of 2007/2008, I have spent a good deal of time managing in turbulent times. The crises I was forced to navigate through often placed at risk the company and its employees' jobs as well as the financial security of my own family. As useful as my experiences from those periods might be, I feel that because they were gained as a result of somewhat traditional economic fluctuations, they are not as illuminating as those lessons that can be obtained from others who have survived far more extreme challenges. I believe this because the lessons learned from the extreme are most often stripped of their veneer of normality and therefore are far more memorable for the student of business history.

Crisis Management in the Extreme

Once extreme positions are analyzed and the resultant lessons extracted, the applicability of those lessons to less radical situations (not to say that these are not terribly painful or injurious) can be made, along with the required adjustments needed to help ensure traditional moral and ethical standards are re-integrated into the lessons in which they might have been omitted due to the severity of the threat to one's personal and financial well being. Therefore, the approach taken for this handbook is to adopt a personal outlook to surviving and preserving one's employment in uber-turbulence.

Surviving in Turbulent Times

Peter Drucker, the father of modern business management,[3] in 1980 opened his classic management text, Managing in Turbulent Times with the following admonition:

> "In turbulent times, an enterprise has to be managed to withstand sudden blows"[4]

Unlike Drucker's work this text is focused not on the survival of the enterprise but rather on the individual needing to survive the "sudden blows" of the turbulence at hand. Thus this work serves as a handbook to assist you in surviving a crisis, not your employer. And if a large corporation employs you, this is definitely not a tutorial in how to help it weather the storm – corporations have the wherewithal to obtain all the support they need from politicians, their legions of lawyers, their accountants, and their own deep pockets or the taxpayer's pockets. If you need proof of the validity of this statement you need look no further than the October 2008 U.S. Government bailout of the major banks. The Troubled Asset Recovery Program (TARP) provided $700 Billion to failing banks while millions of homeowners slipped into the financial hell of mortgage foreclosure.

The Employee's Perspective

As a result of adopting the employee's perspective, I will at times recommend a Machiavellian approach to crisis management, but it is necessary, since the goal here is to provide you with a handbook for occupational self-preservation. Do not expect

1 - Introduction

this book to be your father's or your mother's guide to surviving in turbulent times. The goal of this handbook is to instruct the reader, via a series of lessons in a 'bare knuckles' approach to survival in the jungle we call the marketplace. This is a marketplace where events are not just complicating your business life but are conspiring to destroy your livelihood and your accumulated wealth, as well.

Rationale for the Instructional Approach of this Handbook

To accomplish the instructional goals of this handbook we will examine the decisions and actions of one exceptional survivor who provides us a unique blend of documentary evidence of his business interests, the crises he endured, and his determination to persevere. This individual operated over two thousand years ago, in ancient Rome, not the Rome so often idealized in movies and novels, but rather the Rome of the violent last century before the birth of Christ, when the edifices of the Roman Republic began to fracture and topple. This is the Rome of Julius Caesar, Mark Antony,[5] Marcus Brutus, and Marcus Tullius Cicero, whom a recent biographer labeled as "Rome's greatest politician."[6] This is also the Rome that Cicero himself famously described as a political "cesspool."[7] And among these giants of the tottering ancient Roman Republic operated Titus Pomponius Atticus (referred to in this text as Atticus), a wealthy banker who was especially close to Cicero but also known to Caesar, Antony and Brutus.

Atticus was not just a wealthy banker; he was a businessman with interests in real estate, art,

Career Turbulence

literature, gladiators, history, publishing, and of course, finance, as well as being an author himself. Atticus, in addition to his famous associates and varied interests, was born into the most turbulent of times that also happen to be well documented in the historical record. Therefore by studying Atticus and his experiences we have a unique opportunity to study a businessman who was, in fact, a survivor of extremely turbulent times, and we can extract from his actions numerous lessons of survival that have direct applicability to the economic crises of today.

The Turbulent Times Atticus Endured

Before we begin our detailed study of Atticus and the lessons to be learned from his experiences, it is important first to gain a sense of the degree of turbulence that enveloped Atticus as the Roman Republic collapsed, and thus gain a clear understanding of his value as our role model. Atticus witnessed the rise of political strongmen, years of bloody civil war, and the emergence of the dictator Julius Caesar.

Now, imagine after all that turmoil and bloodshed that Atticus next faced one of the most jarring events in history, the assassination of Julius Caesar on the Ides of March in 44 BC. Not surprisingly, unrest and civil war followed in the wake of Caesar's murder, but Atticus was no mere witness to these events. The banker, Atticus, provided critical financial support to the wife of Mark Antony, Caesar's deputy whom Shakespeare immortalized with his "friends, Romans, countrymen, lend me your ears" speech, while simultaneously lending his financial and moral

1 - Introduction

support to Marcus Brutus, Caesar's lead assassin, a man also immortalized by Shakespeare, to whom the dying Caesar's spoke his last words "et tu Brutus".

One additional complication – Atticus, in his support of Antony was assisting the very politician who would be directly responsible for the brutal execution of Cicero, Atticus' life-long friend. This, then, was not just a difficult stage in world history (and one which we will spend substantially more time dissecting), it was also a deadly juncture for many of the leading participants – so clearly we have a period of time that unquestionably meets the definition of 'turbulent'.

The Condemnation of Atticus by Modern Historians

Finally, after successfully navigating all the turbulence that engulfed his life, Atticus has been criticized by historians and labeled as cowardly.[8] In fact, even the translator of Cicero's letters to Atticus used in this text, D. R. Shackleton Bailey, defended Atticus only by acknowledging how easy it is to be "… less than fair to a man who made so bland a success of safe living in troubled times."[9] Historians, it would seem, find little to praise in a man who survived all the turbulence and destruction of multiple civil wars (when most did not), but demonstrated too little passion in the effort (when passion as exemplified by his friend Cicero brought death), and exhibited too great a passion for financial self-interest (as if those passionately committed to the waging of civil war were doing so only for the most altruistic of reasons). And so the reality is that Atticus did in fact endure all the chaos imagined above and even prospered in the process.

Career Turbulence

Atticus was a talented man trying day-to-day literally to hold on to his head and to protect his family and his livelihood from the depredations of far more powerful and ruthless men. This, then, is why the life of Atticus is an ideal case study, for Atticus the businessman managed to survive when all of the aforementioned powerbrokers of such historical significance did not.

Atticus' Position in Society

Atticus' societal position as a wealthy businessman can be seen in Figure 1.3 depicting the social hierarchy of ancient Rome. Note: Atticus as an aristocratic businessman was part of the upper class of Romans known as equestrians or knights, but were subordinate in status to the politically active Senators. Consuls and former consuls were considered the elite of the Senatorial class. In the Roman Republic two Consuls were typically elected annually. The Consulship was the most powerful and prestigious elected office in the Republic. Together, the equestrians and the Senators comprised the aristocracy of the Roman Republic.

1 - Introduction

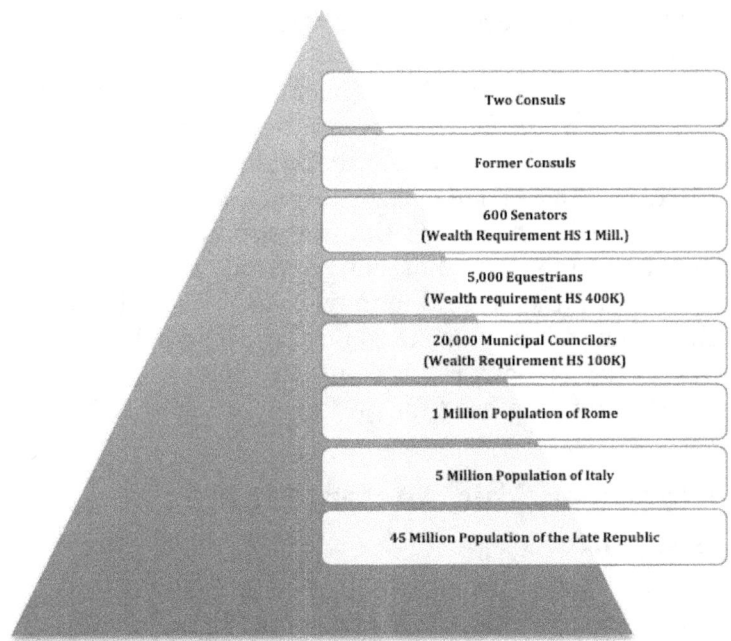

Figure 1.3: Shows Atticus' position as a very wealthy equestrian in the late Republic. (Note: The population figures for the equestrians, councilors, and the population of Rome as well as Italy come from the early years of the Roman Empire, a period shortly after Atticus' death, and an age in which we have significantly more detailed census data).[10]

Atticus as a Role Model in a Crisis

The lessons to be gained from such a man and his amazing ability to survive are timeless and therefore of great importance for any individual today who finds himself or herself in need of an experienced guide to help navigate through the darkness of today's uncertain business terrain. We will look beyond the distaste of some historians and use Atticus as a source of wisdom, despite his occasional

Career Turbulence

moral lapses. Perhaps if Shakespeare had also helped immortalize Atticus as he did Antony and Brutus (Caesar and Cicero needed no Shakespeare), the world would have a greater sensitivity and appreciation for his accomplishments. But I fear not, for Atticus suffers from a greater historical disadvantage than most politicians - the disadvantage of the labels he actually earned – banker, financier, and moneylender – tags that allow the owner of such terms to be presumed self-serving and guilty of 'back room deals' in which all are potentially sacrificed for profit.

Atticus and his Ancient Literary Supporters

Atticus, despite the distaste of some historians, does have one literary heavyweight in his corner. For the great Cicero, author, politician, lawyer, and orator whose works influenced the Renaissance as well as America's Founding Fathers,[11] declared that Atticus was closer to him than a brother, and left us over 400 relatively unvarnished letters that he had written to Atticus on events large and small, touching upon both public and private matters. These letters were written between 68 BC and 43 BC and provide Cicero's first hand insights into the fall of the Roman Republic,[12] a period in which he was a major actor.

Atticus also has in his corner Cornelius Nepos, his "unexciting but competent" biographer who was a friend,[13] admirer, and certainly not an unbiased source (see Appendix A for more background on Nepos). Nepos surprisingly wrote his biography of Atticus while Atticus still lived.[14] Given that Atticus

1 - Introduction

had a friendship with Nepos and that Atticus was alive at the time of the Nepos' publication of the biography's first edition, it is not unreasonable to assume that Atticus himself might have contributed to and even vetted portions of the work. Therefore it is likely that Nepos' biographical sketch offers the reader a perspective into the way Atticus wanted to be remembered. This of course does not ensure that we have an accurate history of Atticus' life or his deeds and so we must remain vigilant and recognize that there may be times when Nepos the friend of Atticus manipulated the facts to suit his literary purposes.

Given that we must be careful with the Atticus as presented by Nepos, the best means of balancing Nepos' rendition of Atticus' life is through the extant letters of Cicero. Those letters perhaps provide our best opportunity to find the real Atticus, and so the weaving together of the portraits left by both Nepos and Cicero offer us a richer and more faithful portrayal of Atticus that can be obtained from Nepos alone.

Background on the Rise of the Roman Republic

Before we begin our study of Atticus and his survival during the collapse of the Roman Republic, we must first briefly review the legend of the Republic's rise.[15] It is important to remember that the Roman Republic and its institutions of government had already flourished for more than four centuries before Atticus and his ambitious contemporaries arrived on the scene. The Roman's placed the date of the

Career Turbulence

founding of the city of Rome at 753 BC but that early city-state was ruled by kings for nearly two and a half centuries before the Republic's creation.

It was not until 509 BC that Lucius Junius Brutus led a revolt that ended the rule of kings and initiated the founding of the Roman Republic. Additionally this Brutus, as one of Rome's first consuls, forced the citizens of the new Roman Republic to swear an oath that there would never be allowed another king in Rome. When Lucius Junius Brutus' own sons were found to have conspired to restore the monarchy, he ordered their death and stoically watched their execution. In the early Republic, to help avoid the emergence of another king, male citizens would elect two consuls with 'king-like' power, but limited to a single one-year term. In the late Republic these consular restrictions eroded with catastrophic results.

Figure 1.4: A 1789 painting by Jacques-Louis David that depicts Lucius Junius Brutus receiving the bodies of his two sons that he condemned to death for plotting to restore the monarchy.[16]

1 - Introduction

Background on the Fall of the Roman Republic

That early and steadfast commitment to a republican government played no small role in the Roman Republic's birth and its death nearly half a millennium later. Over the more than four hundred intervening years that spanned the life of the Republic, Rome -- through its military triumphs -- grew into the greatest empire the world had seen. Born into the Republic as it was ascending to its widest geographical extent was Atticus in 109 BC, as well as his future friend and correspondent Cicero in 106 BC. Antony Everitt wrote in his 2003 biography of Cicero that at the time of Cicero and Atticus' birth, the Roman Republic appeared to be:

> "... at the height of its power and wealth. It controlled a vast empire that stretched from Spain to Asia Minor. No serious external threat was in sight or could be imagined. However, behind the façade of this magnificent edifice the internal structure was unsound. The walls could not bear the weight they were carrying. Sooner or later collapse was inevitable." [17]

The causes of the fractures of that "magnificent edifice" are complex but a few of the "hammer blows" to the structure of the Republic can be readily discerned and are listed below and depicted in Figure 1.5.

Career Turbulence

1. The creation of a professional army with greater allegiance to its commanders than the state.
2. The paralysis of the Roman Senate due to the evolution of powerful factions and the rise of political strongmen.
3. The recognition that the mob and violence could be useful to gaining and retaining political power.
4. Political office becoming a vehicle for personal gain.

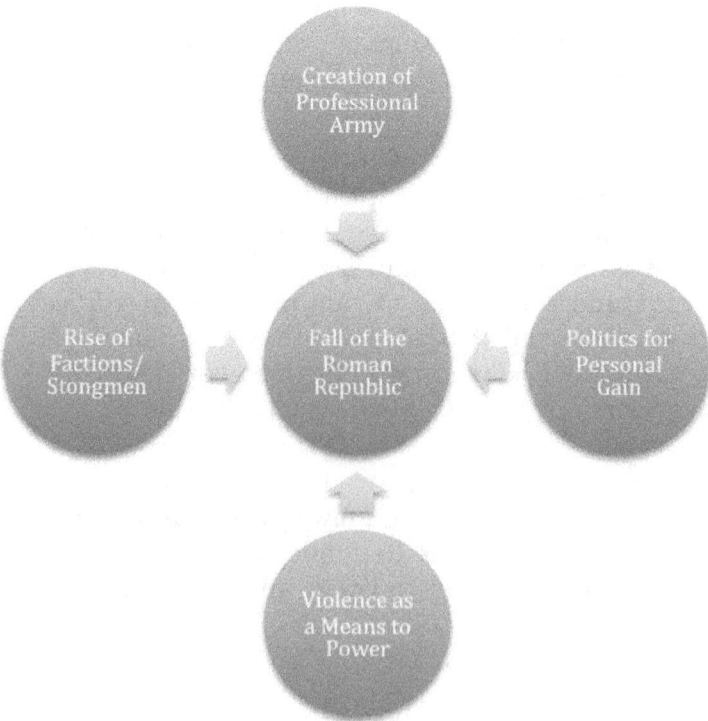

Figure 1.5: Shows four major hammer blows to the Roman Republic that ultimately led to civil war and the fall of the Republic.

1 - Introduction

The Inevitability of Collapse

In hindsight, of course, it is easy now to say that the fall of the Republic was inevitable, but at the time of Cicero and Atticus' birth after centuries of stability, such a collapse certainly was not considered inevitable and more likely would not even have been considered.

However, in the ensuing decades of the lives of Atticus and Cicero, the potential for collapse of the republic moved from hypothetical to real as civil discourse faltered and political conflicts fell into cycles of rigidity, then violence, and thrice into full-scale civil war. What follows is the story of that chaotic and bloody spiral that ended the Roman Republic and in its place substituted Imperial Rome, a system of government led by an Emperor with unlimited power and an emasculated Senate. The complex and painful process of that metamorphosis would stretch over most of a century and consume countless lives. But included on the long list of the dead would not be the name of Atticus.

Two Cautions Before We Begin

As discussed above, the actions of Atticus' that helped ensure his survival can best be discerned by combining the facts and inferences that comprised the public image making left by Nepos with elements from Cicero's private letters to Atticus. We should note however, that many of Cicero's later letters were written at times of great peril, and some were on occasion subject to self-censorship (see Appendix C for more detail on Cicero's self-censorship).
It also appears that "Cicero's anxiety over the confidentiality of his correspondence extended into

Career Turbulence

the future, and toward the end of his life he began to betray a concern to leave an edited and sanitized corpus of letters for posterity." [18]

Additionally, it is probable that Atticus destroyed letters from Cicero that were unduly compromising.[19] Thus we have great insight into Atticus from Cicero's letters yet we must be cautious and recognize that at times we may be examining details relevant to the events under discussion by Cicero, but that they may have been "sanitized".

A second caution with regard to Atticus' is also required. Earlier we saw Atticus described as "bland". The reality is that Atticus lived in a time that has captured the imagination of succeeding civilizations and the major players left such an impact on the pages of history that it is not surprising that Atticus pales in comparison to his more colorful compatriots. The key for us, though, is not to lament Atticus' absence of fame and glory, but rather admire his passion for survival, and the lessons that we can coax from that passion.

Author's Note: A timeline of the life of Atticus is shown in Figure 1.6a. A descriptive list of ancient Romans found in the timeline of the life of Atticus can be found in Figure 1.6b.

1 - Introduction

Date (BC)	Major Event	Age of Atticus
109	Birth of Atticus	Born
106	Birth of Cicero	3
100	Birth of Caesar	9
99	Birth of Nepos	10
88-82	Sulla's Civil War with Marius	21-27
86/85	Death of Atticus' Father Atticus Leaves Rome for Athens	23 / 24
82-81	Dictatorship of Sulla	27-28
65	Atticus Returns to Rome	44
63	Cicero Elected Consul (Roman Republic's Highest Office) Birth of Octavius	46
60	Republic Led by Caesar, Pompey and Crassus. (Called the First Triumvirate)	49
58	Cicero Exiled Atticus Inherits 10M Sesterces from Caecilius	51
57	Cicero's Return from Exile	52
56	Atticus Marries Pilia	53
54	Death of Julia, Caesar's daughter, Pompey's Wife	55
53	Crassus Killed in Parthia	56
49	Caesar's Civil War Begins	60
48	Caesar's Defeat of Pompey Dictatorship of Caesar Begins	61
47	Caesar Pardons Cicero for Supporting Pompey	62

Career Turbulence

44	Caesar's Assassination Conspiracy Led by Brutus and Cassius Octavius Adopted by Caesar in his Will (Octavius referred to from this period forward as Octavian) Mark Antony Becomes Consul Death of Atticus' Wife Pilia Early Stages of Civil War	65
43	Cicero Executed	66
42	Defeat and Suicide of Brutus and Cassius Empire Led by Octavian, Antony and Lepidus (Called the Second Triumvirate)	67
37	Atticus' Daughter Marries Agrippa	72
32	Death of Atticus	77

Figure 1.6a: Shows a timeline of the life of Atticus with the dates of major events leading up to the fall of the Roman Republic as well Atticus' approximate age at each of the events.[20]

1 - Introduction

Name	Description
Agrippa, (c. 64/63 BC-12 BC)	Friend and loyal lieutenant of Octavian, married Atticus' daughter.
Antony, (83 BC-30 BC)	served under Caesar, consul 44 B.C., triumvir with Octavian and Lepidus
Brutus, (85 BC-42 BC)	leading conspirator in Caesar's assassination, friend of Atticus
Caecilius, (c. 130 BC-58 BC)	wealthy uncle of Atticus
Caesar, (100 BC-44 BC)	consul 59 BC, triumvir with Pompey and Crassus, dictator 49 BC – 44 BC, assassinated on March 15, 44 BC
Cassius, (c. 85 BC-42 BC)	leading conspirator in Caesar's assassination
Cicero, (106 BC-43 BC)	consul 63 BC, author, politician, lawyer, orator, lifelong friend of Atticus, executed in 43 BC
Crassus, (115 BC-53 BC)	consul 70 BC and 55 BC, triumvir with Caesar and Pompey
Julia, (c. 83 BC-54 BC)	daughter of Julius Caesar, Pompey's wife
Lepidus, (c. 89/88 BC-13/12 BC)	consul in 46 BC, triumvir with Mark Antony and Octavian
Marius, (157 BC-86 BC)	consul 107 BC, 104 BC - 100 BC, 86 BC, former commanding officer of Sulla and later opponent in civil war
Nepos (c. 99 BC-24 BC)	biographer of Atticus

Career Turbulence

Octavian, (63 BC-14 AD)	adopted son of Caesar, triumvir with Mark Antony and Lepidus, later Emperor Augustus
Pilia, (c. 75 BC-44 BC)	wife of Atticus
Pompey, (106 BC-48 BC)	consul 70 BC, 55 BC and 52 BC, triumvir with Caesar and Crassus
Sulla, (c. 138 BC-78 BC)	consul 88 BC and 82 BC, dictator 82-79 BC, early admirer of the youthful Atticus

Figure 1.6b: Shows a discriptive list of the ancient Romans listed in Figure 1.6a

CHAPTER 2

The Early Life of Atticus

Timeline for Major Events in this Chapter (109 BC-85 BC)

Date (BC)	Major Event	Age of Atticus
109	Birth of Atticus	Born
106	Birth of Cicero	3
100	Birth of Caesar	9
99	Birth of Nepos	10
88-82	Sulla's Civil War with Marius	21-27
86/85	Death of Atticus' Father Atticus Leaves Rome for Athens	23/24

Period Background

As the Roman Republic was to enter its final century, major political fissures split the state's ruling aristocracy. For centuries, the politically active senators and business-oriented equestrians had successfully guided the Roman Republic. Although there were often heated debates upon the issues of the day, those disputes had historically only rarely exploded into violence. However, as the republic expanded (see Figure 2.1), and as huge numbers of slaves along with great wealth flowed into the hands of the Roman aristocracy, willingness to compromise declined while the propensity for settling political feuds through violence increased.

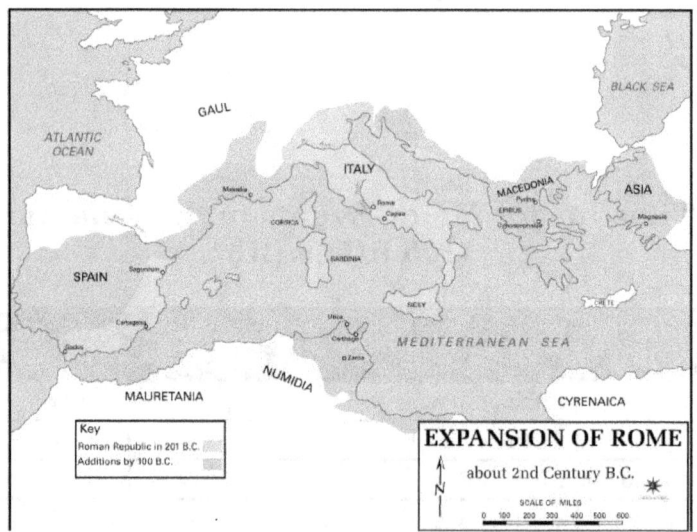

Figure 2.1: Shows the expansion of the Roman Republic from 200 BC to 100 BC. This is the extent of the Republic near the time of Atticus' birth.[21]

The Rise of Factions

In this unsettled climate two factions emerged and though their membership was somewhat dynamic the chasm between their positions continued to widen over time until civil upheavals and violence ensued. Violence, of course, spawned more violence until civil war became inevitable. These two factions

2 - The Early Life of Atticus

were known then (and today) as the "Optimates" or "best men" and the "Populares" or "favoring the people." Although it is not an ideal comparison, these two groups can be considered something akin to modern conservatives and liberals/progressives where the conservatives are focused on a minimalist approach to societal changes and the liberals/progressives seek more substantive transformations in traditional institutions and governmental policies. But the similarities stopped there. The Optimates and Populares of the Roman Republic were both comprised of aristocrats - Senators, equestrians and their extended clans, and unlike their modern day party equivalents, members of these factions often had significant familial relationships with each other, through marriage or social connections, with the result that there was much more fluidity to the formation and maintenance of each group's so called membership.

It is important to point out that Senators, as the elite of the aristocracy, were restricted from many forms of commerce (much of which was considered vulgar and beneath a gentleman.)[22] Senators were specifically excluded from banking. For senators, conquest, political office, and the agricultural business of great landed estates were thought to be the most honorable means of wealth accretion. The less haughty equestrians, on the other hand, were the mainspring of non-agricultural business such as shipping, mining, commerce, tax farming,[23] and of course banking.

Career Turbulence

The Rise of Sulla

The first great upheaval between the Optimates and the Populares, with civil strife culminating in a civil war, occurred when Atticus was in his early twenties. Emerging victorious from that carnage was a Senator, general, and politician by the name of Lucius Cornelius Sulla who was very much a Roman traditionalist and a member of the Optimates. Sulla used his battled hardened Roman Legions to march on Rome (this was the first time that a Roman general had ever marched on his own capital).

Figure 2.2: Shows a marble bust of Lucius Cornelius Sulla a Roman Senator who used the troops under his command to march on Rome.[24]

2 - The Early Life of Atticus

Atticus Endangered by his Uncle's Actions

Unfortunately for Atticus an uncle named Sulpicius played a significant role in fomenting the political instability that fomented Sulla's march on Rome,[25] but he did so in support of the faction (Populares) opposed to Sulla and led at the time by one of Rome's greatest generals, Gaius Marius. Marius was Sulla's former commanding officer and was also responsible for transforming the Roman legions from a citizen army into a professional army (helping to accelerate the fall of the Republic as soldiers became more loyal to their commanding officers rather than the state). Marius was also the first Roman to serve as consul seven times.

The result of Sulpicius' support for the faction led by Marius was that Sulpicius lost his life in the ensuing violence,[26] and young Atticus, merely because he was related by marriage to Sulpicius, was also at risk of losing his life and family estates as well.[27] With this background in mind now let's move on to Nepos and his depiction of Atticus' early life and times.

Career Turbulence

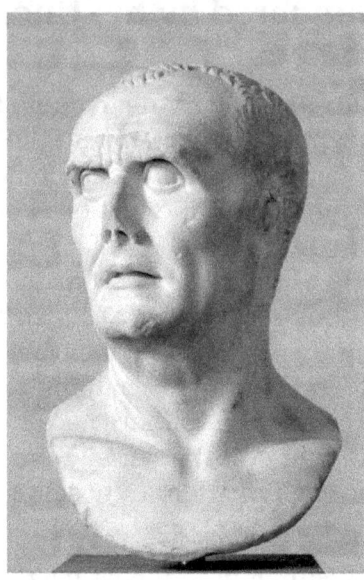

Figure 2.3: Shows a marble bust of Gaius Marius, the first Roman to serve as consul seven times and who, via what where known as the Marian Reforms, established a professional army. These reforms were to play a critical role in the demise of the Roman Republic. [28]

Nepos on the Family of Atticus[29]

(1.1) "Titus Pomponius Atticus, descended from the most ancient Roman stock, never abandoned the equestrian rank which he had inherited from his ancestors."

(1.2) "His father was attentive to business and rich for those days."[30]

Nepos in his opening sentence (1.1) is first and foremost establishing the aristocratic equestrian credentials of Atticus by indicating the antiquity of his lineage (which supposedly went back as far

2 - The Early Life of Atticus

as the time of Roman kings). The prestige of one's ancestry was extraordinarily important to the Romans and especially to Roman aristocrats, with some taking their line of descent much further back, such as Julius Caesar who claimed descent from the goddess Venus.

Interestingly, Nepos emphasizes that Atticus "never abandoned" his equestrian rank. This phrasing makes a virtue of the fact that Atticus never sought political office nor became a Senator. In Republican Rome there was great honor associated in climbing to Rome's highest offices and aristocrats were expected to do so – failure to seek advancement was viewed by the elite with disdain, and so here we see Nepos explaining Atticus' actions as a 'positive' when many would have viewed his decision to remain a "mere" businessman as a negative.

In ancient Rome it was also honorable to follow in the footsteps of one's father, and so by establishing Atticus' father's business credentials early, in sentence 1.2, Atticus can be seen as honoring his father and his family by continuing with the family's business interests (and not abandoning them for the Senate). In other words, Nepos wants his readers to know that, when Atticus begins to dabble in the business of banking, he did not just decide to pursue business interests of his own account but he did so out of filial devotion to honor family tradition. We should note here the absence of any detail from Nepos as to what comprised the business interests of Atticus' family.

Career Turbulence

The Family Wealth of Atticus

The second phrase in sentence 1.2 is interesting because Nepos positions Atticus' father as "rich for those days". If we assume "those days" of Atticus' father's refers to the time around the birth of Atticus in 109 BC we can draw two conclusions as to what Nepos is alluding to:

1. During the late Republic the benchmark for being wealthy moved higher as money and slaves flowed into Rome.

2. The business success and wealth of Atticus, the son, would eclipse that of his father, who was merely "rich for those days" – increasing the dignity and prestige of both Atticus and his family.

Nepos Accentuates the Positive

A key point to be drawn from this initial section of Atticus' biography and useful for any businessperson to remember in any period, whether turbulent or not, is the need to accentuate the positive and to do so aggressively. Atticus would have wished right from the start to be viewed in a positive light, and Nepos does not disappoint. As we see here and shall see as his narrative progresses, Nepos continually builds upon his opening section until a glowing panegyric is fully constructed, smothering critics and those of faint praise alike. Given that Nepos' biography is literature's earliest surviving example of a living person's biography, and despite frequent criticism of the author, Nepos forged on Atticus' behalf a now very well worn literary path taken by many individuals over the last two millennia – maximizing one's virtues while minimizing the vices.

2 - The Early Life of Atticus

Lesson 1: Self-promotion is no Vice

This initial job preservation lesson to be learned from Atticus' life is perhaps better phrased by the famed economist John Kenneth Galbraith, a professor at both Harvard and Princeton who served in a variety of governmental offices under several presidents including John F. Kennedy (once a student of Galbraith's at Harvard). Galbraith, no shrinking violet (and at a towering 6'8" and the author of 33 books on economics, it would have been difficult for him to be described as such),[31] according to The Economist kept a framed sampler in his home in Cambridge, MA to remind his visitors that: "Modesty is a vastly overrated virtue." [32]

Figure 2.4: This 1961 photo shows a towering John Kenneth Galbraith (at far left as Kennedy's Ambassador to India) with President Kennedy and Vice President Johnson.

Career Turbulence

Lesson Summary

In any discussion of professional capabilities, as Galbraith well knew, it is definitely not a virtue to sell yourself short – and keep in mind that your competition will always be more than willing to assist in that respect. Remember not to damn yourself with faint praise since in tough times it can be difficult to be seen as a key player so step up and step up often so as to make yourself indispensible (or at least appear indispensible).

Nepos on the Education of Atticus

(1.3) "He ... trained his son in all the studies essential for the education of the young. Moreover, the boy had ... a capacity for learning."

(1.4) "(Schoolmates) were Lucius Torquatus, the younger Gaius Marius, and Marcus Cicero with all of whom he became so intimate that as long as he lived no one was dearer to him."

Sections 1.3 and 1.4 inform the reader that the proper education of Atticus was important to his father and that Atticus had the opportunity to learn with other students who were either sons' of Rome's elite at that time (Lucius Torquatus was a descendent of an very ancient and powerful family that claimed numerous consuls; the younger Gaius Marius was the adopted son of the seven time consul Marius discussed above) or those who would eventually become Rome's elite themselves (such as Cicero).

These schoolboy connections Atticus nurtured and kept for a lifetime. By doing do so Atticus

2 - The Early Life of Atticus

displayed great fidelity as well as gaining the not insignificant additional benefit of raising his perceived status in society. For in ancient Rome, both family and friends were important to a man's prestige. Thus Nepos establishes for his readers that Atticus was not only of illustrious descent, true to his family and a friend to Rome's most eminent men but also committed himself to a quality education.

Lesson 2: Cultivate the Powerful

A commitment to education is of course extraordinarily important, but, the key take away for us from this section of Nepos' biography is that if you wish to lever yourself up from your current station in life, and to extend your influence, **it is critical to cultivate the more powerful whenever feasible**. This lesson has even found its way to one of the modern world's richest men, Warren Buffet. Buffet wrote in a New York Times Op-Ed piece, albeit a bit tongue in cheek, that: "It's nice to have friends in high places."[34]

Figure 2.5: Shows Warren Buffet with President Barack Obama.[35]

Career Turbulence

Lesson Summary

Often stated as something of a mantra, but far less frequently implemented with the success demonstrated by Atticus, this lesson requires constant diligence in order to effectively spread a network of associates ever wider and ever higher. A well-constructed network of influential associates not only becomes a potential springboard for success but in difficult times can be a priceless job safety net, as well.

The development of influential friendships outside your circle takes energy, dedication and most importantly the willingness to stay in touch but the rewards can be huge. Two of Atticus' childhood friends became consuls of the Roman Republic and Atticus' influence grew accordingly. Whether Atticus profited directly or indirectly from his friends in powerful positions is irrelevant, more importantly for us is that Atticus created the opportunity to profit (e.g. important appointments for associates, lucrative contracts, letters of introduction, influence in policy debates, and an ever widening network of powerful aristocrats) by simply reaching out to and staying in touch with associates from his youth.

Nepos on Tragedy and Strategy

(2.1) "His father died early."

(2.2) "(Atticus) when a mere youth ... because he was related by marriage to Sulpicius ... was involved in some danger ... No opportunity was given him of living as his rank demanded without offending one or the other faction (in the civil war between Sulla and Marius) ... he thought it a favorable opportunity for gratifying his tastes, and went to Athens."

2 - The Early Life of Atticus

(2.3) "And in order that his sojourn abroad might not inflict any loss upon his property, he transported a great part of his fortune to Athens."

We learn in this section that Atticus' father died young, perhaps in 86 BC when Atticus was in his early twenties (and civil war raged).[36] We learn from Nepos elsewhere in his biography of Atticus that Atticus inherited from his father, who was wealthy for "those days", two million sesterces (approximately $8 Million).[37] We can assume this was the bulk of Atticus' father estate but cannot know the amount that was in illiquid assets such as real estate.

Atticus Threatened

We are next informed by Nepos that Atticus was in substantial danger because of the actions of Sulpicius and that Atticus was left "no opportunity" to live as "his rank demanded" without offending one faction or the other. Sulpicius had offended Sulla's faction, and this clearly produced the direct threat to Atticus. According to Nepos, the threat was sufficiently severe – this period saw significant political upheaval that resulted in civil war – that the actions of Sulpicius would have forced Atticus to the side of Marius operating against Sulla unless Atticus vacated the scene – which he did. We should note that if Atticus stayed in Rome and failed to side with Marius' faction, that faction too would have been offended.

Career Turbulence

Atticus Departs for Athens to Avoid Choosing Sides

Nepos next says that Atticus departed for Athens in order to gratify his tastes e.g. his love for Greek learning, culture, and art. (We should note here that Nepos merely provides Atticus' full name in the opening sentence of his biography without mentioning where the name Atticus had come from; it was simply adopted by Atticus after his residency in Athens,[38] as Atticus wanted to demonstrate his great affinity for all things Hellenistic. Today we might call Atticus' self-choice of such a name posturing, but in his time it was acceptable, especially given Atticus' fluency in Greek, his decision to reside in Athens for what was to be a long residency and the services he would render the Athenians.)

Atticus may have chosen Athens because of his love of all things Greek, but his choice of a departure time is also indicative of a strong desire to avoid the risk of choosing sides in a war where one faction would win and the other side likely destroyed. Flight offered the best opportunity for guaranteed survival and wealth preservation.

Atticus' Withdrawal From Rome

We should recognize Atticus' strategic withdrawal from the pending conflagration as nothing less than brilliant. **For in not choosing sides Atticus demonstrated that he was willing to forgo the potential opportunity to gain more (if he chose a side that won) and endure the risk to his reputation (e.g. being labeled a coward) if**

2 - The Early Life of Atticus

there was a chance of drawing a losing hand. As we shall see later, this was a strategy Atticus was to employ again and again. However, this was the first instance and so all the more insightful because he did not act based upon a personal precedent or experience but rather his decision was wisely formulated and executed at a remarkably young age by someone who we should also assume was grieving over a deceased father (from whom a significant inheritance funded both Atticus' decision to leave Rome and his future banking endeavors).

The youthful Atticus recognized he was in a difficult position in a very dangerous time. Too often in a crisis even the experienced manager or executive will ignore or dismiss an initial sense of foreboding with calamitous results. Atticus did not ignore the risks of staying or the discomfort and difficulties of leaving his established life. Atticus made the critical decision to depart from Rome for Athens to ensure his personal safety. A crucial tactic of self-preservation emerges from this section of Atticus' biography - Atticus recognized he could not guarantee his own security through an alignment with the faction of Sulpicius, so he executed a strategy of self-preservation in the only fashion he could, by vacating Rome.

Lesson 3: Get the Hell out of Dodge

The lesson gained from Atticus' strategic exit is not often applied in the business world. Far too often the intention is to stay and battle for survival. A timely exit is seen as not being tough enough, and even construed as weakness. However, there are times when "toughing it out" is simply not the right

Career Turbulence

strategy for career survival. Perhaps one of the most emphatic articulations of the need to make a timely exit is advice given to John Travolta's troubled character in the movie *Pulp Fiction* where Travolta's character was wisely advised by Winston "The Wolf" Wolfe (played by Harvey Keitel) that it was time to "...get the fuck out of Dodge." [39]

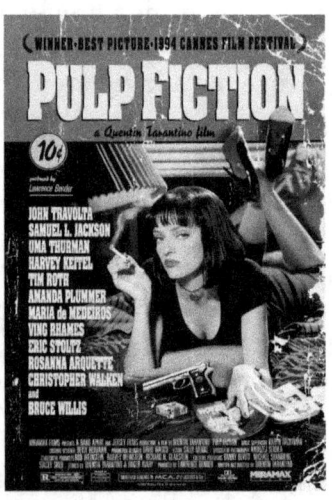

Figure 2.6: Shows a poster from the movie Pulp Fiction.[40] *(Copyright Miramax/Courtesy Everett Collection)*

Lesson Summary

When in a battle in which you are politically outmanned, out influenced, or unduly vulnerable, there is no sin in exiting the scene and attempting to avoid a major conflict. Absence in these instances can be a virtue, allowing the turmoil to blow over and permitting you to survive when active participation might be political suicide. Atticus removed himself from Rome to Athens, and in

2 - The Early Life of Atticus

today's corporate environment, depending on the depth and duration of the problem as well as the size of your company, you can choose to travel to visit customers and other employees, take a vacation, enjoy a sabbatical, make a timely job change or if at all possible, like Atticus, relocate. All of these options are too often overlooked or unfortunately examined only at the last moment. Always plan ahead for a disaster, and if a physical departure is not feasible, establish a back-up plan that minimizes the impact of staying put, but by all means have a strategy, and remember that burying your head in the sand is not a plan for long-term or even short-term survival.

Atticus and his Assets

In the section above we also see another prudent act taken by Atticus: he "transported a great part of his fortune to Athens". We should understand an important point here. In antiquity, as most of the Roman elite had their wealth tied up in vast estates that were hardly liquid assets, a geographic transfer of a significant portion of a personal fortune (in this case the inheritance of two million sesterces) most likely meant that those assets had to be changed into coin or precious metal in order to be moved.

To sell real estate required time (and still does), and one could imagine that selling any assets in a time of civil unrest required both dexterity and diligence in order to avoid being forced to dump property at fire sale prices. We can therefore assume that Atticus required some time to move his property once he decided to sell, but that he did not have the luxury of waiting too long for the best price,

Career Turbulence

since the longer he waited to sell, the greater the risk became of not removing himself from Rome. In summary, we see that that Atticus fully recognized he was in a period of high risk, that he should be "long" in cash, and "short" in physical assets.

Lesson 4: Cash is King

For the modern business person, especially in troubled times, sufficient cash on hand and minimum debt is often the best means to ensure a freedom of movement that would be closed to a wage earner who could only survive by utilizing credit and incurring additional debt. The lesson from Atticus' actions in his time of crisis is always to remember and operationalize the old adage that, "cash is king." [41]

Figure 2.7: This photo is an intended as a reminder that you are never too young to remember the old adage that cash is king, especially in periods of great upheaval.[42] (Copyright Andresr/ Shutterstock.com)

2 - The Early Life of Atticus

Lesson Summary

In a crisis such as a lost job, credit is often impossible to come by (and even if you had a job, banks simply refused to loan money during the debt crisis of 2008). Additionally personal debt, — especially credit card debt — is expensive to sustain, hence the timeless wisdom of Atticus' decision to hoard his cash in a troubled time. At the risk of becoming repetitive, if a prolonged downturn in personal fortune is expected or even just merely suspected, make sure, wherever feasible, to convert hard assets into cash (e.g. downsize the family home, sell the vacation place, boat, or the extra car) in order to pay down any existing debts and if possible, to keep sufficient cash on hand to withstand any "blows."

Atticus Relocates to a War Zone

By choosing Athens, however, Atticus was moving into a recently active war zone. For Sulla had besieged Athens in 87 BC, so it hardly makes sense for Atticus to have moved there until after operations had ceased and Sulla had moved on to other targets in Asia. This would place Atticus' move to Athens to around 86/85 BC and his age at 23 or 24. The rewards for Atticus following Sulla's war machine into Athens would have been many. As a member of the Roman aristocracy, Atticus would have been in a position to benefit from the destruction,[43] especially given his now readily available hoard of cash and the freedom allowed a particularly well connected equestrian citizen of Rome (such as guaranteeing loans). Professor Kathryn E. Welch, in her 1996 article, "T.

Career Turbulence

Pomponius Atticus: A Banker in Politics?" made just this point when she writes:

> "In a country torn by war and financial disaster and with less competition than he would perhaps normally have had, Atticus had a reasonably clear field for enormous profit." [44]

Clearly a wise decision by Atticus was to go where the competition (i.e. other bankers) didn't appear to have a strong foothold -- or if they did, where they might have alienated their clients by charging exorbitant rates of interest (certainly something not unusual for either ancient or modern bankers).

Nepos on Atticus and the Athenians

(2.4) "(Atticus) ... often relieved their (the Athenian government's) public necessities by his wealth. For example, when the state needed to negotiate a loan and could not do so on fair terms, he always came to the rescue, and in a way that he never exacted from them excessive interest, nor would he allow them to remain in debt beyond the stipulated time."

(2.5) "And both those conditions were to their advantage, since he did not by indulgence allow their debt to grow old, nor yet to increase by the piling up of interest."

Sections 2.4 and 2.5 above now bring for the first time a lens to the early financing activity of Atticus. We see he is not loaning money to mere individuals here, but to the Athenian government itself. As mentioned earlier, this was a benefit of being a Roman citizen living in a war-damaged city such as Athens. Loans to the state would have been significant in size and Nepos emphasizes the magnanimity of Atticus' terms of credit with the city – no rapacious interest and timely repayment as compared to the competition which Nepos tells us was offering high rates of interest and allowing debts to age beyond contracted due dates.

Atticus: Financier to the Athenians

Nepos is effusive on how beneficial Atticus' terms to the war ravaged Greeks were, for Atticus avoided the undue aging of debts which really is a kind way of saying that Atticus did not tolerate deadbeats as clients and eschewed the application of exorbitant interest rates (which were, at least in theory, precluded by Roman law anyway). It should also be remembered that fairness is often very dependent on perspective and a desperate client might accept any terms, even if they were only a bit better than the others, to stave off financial ruin in the short term. There is an old saying that a drowning man will cling to a blade of grass and perhaps that applies here, for in their desperation the Athenian clients of Atticus might have called any interest rate improvement fair, if that was the best they could obtain following Sulla's siege of the city.

We should note that by offering terms that avoided the appearance of "excessive" interest, Atticus was not just being altruistic (as Nepos would have us believe), but rather he recognized that in better times other competitive financiers might step in with lower rates, and therefore fairness in difficult times would help ensure that the citizens of Athens would remain his clients into the future.

Lesson 5: Firmness is not Synonymous with Abrasiveness

The operational approach adopted by Atticus in this instance was not to avoid toughness, especially in unsettled times, but rather to avoid being so visibly tough that his business was weakened, not strengthened. Intimidation in the workplace of peers or subordinates (if in management) is not the best means to create a positive reputation and more often than not can damage or end a career. Therefore the more effective you are at masking a firm approach the more likely the achievement of your work-related goals. This lesson of knowing when to mask steely deeds with kind words and works was advocated by Napoleon Bonaparte who emerged from the turmoil of the French Revolution as the Emperor of France and advised, "Put your iron hand in a velvet glove."[45]

2 - The Early Life of Atticus

Figure 2.8: Shows Napoleon Bonaparte, Emperor of the French and the King of Italy in an 1812 painting by Jacques-Louis David. [46]

Lesson Summary

We see that Atticus, after liquidating his assets and departing Rome for Athens, did not attempt to increase his wealth quickly in a rapacious fashion, but pursued his goals via a longer-term vision and a more gentle hand. Please note that this advice to disguise a firmness of action within a veil of mildness works best and longest if the harsh decisions are in fact the last resort and not the first.

Career Turbulence

Nepos on the Generosity of Atticus

(2.6) "He (Atticus) added to this service another act of generosity; for he made a distribution of grain to the entire people (of Athens)."

In sentence 2.6 we see that Nepos further enhances the reputation of Atticus by following the interest rate discussion with the publicizing of an act of generosity by Atticus to his clients. We see a similar strategy in today's marketplace where companies are quick to shout their good deeds from the rooftops, especially when they are concerned with buttressing a reputation, quelling the concerns about misdeeds, or countering bad press (e.g. BP advertising after the oil spill in the Gulf of Mexico). The act of providing grain to a war-torn city's citizens was truly generous on Atticus' part. Nepos (and very possibly Atticus) would have wanted his readers to know that.

Cicero's Comments on the Generosity of Atticus

Nepos' phrasing appears to indicate that the grain distribution was done only once ("a distribution") and is situated by Nepos in the biography in such a way so that the generous action on Atticus' part appears to be at a time not long after Atticus arrived in Athens (the mid-80's BC). Fortunately, we also have for the first time in this study, Cicero's comments on an event depicted in the biography. In a letter to Atticus, Cicero ribbed his close friend, "But what's all this? Panem populo (bread for the people) at Athens? Do you think that is in order? Not that my volumes have anything against it, since it

2 - The Early Life of Atticus

was not a largesse (a bribe) to fellow countrymen but a piece of generosity to foreign hosts." [47]

Given that the donation was to foreigners (e.g. non-Romans) it was not a political bribe on Atticus' part, but the jab by Cicero certainly hinted the action resembled a bribe. And although we see that Cicero confirms that the (very generous) distribution actually took place, there is an independent means of dating the time of the donation by the date of Cicero's letter to Atticus referencing the event. The letter from Cicero to Atticus that discusses the donation was not from the 80's BC but rather written in 55 BC, more than a quarter of a century later than the time implied by Nepos' retelling of the incident!

Lesson 6: Do not Dismiss the Value of an Occasional Overstatement

In this instance Nepos cleverly references a later event at the same time that he is discussing earlier events – there is no erroneous reporting - the timing is simply inferred to be proximate by the reader. Despite Nepos' generous concatenation of events, he has constructed his praise of Atticus on a foundation of truth (e.g. Atticus did make a very significant donation to the citizenry of Athens). However, the lesson from this literary slight of hand is to do as Donald Trump, one of the great businessmen and marketers of our generation advised, and remember that, "... a little hyperbole now and then never hurts." [48]

Career Turbulence

Figure 2.9: This photo shows Donald Trump, a businessman who has never been shy about utilizing "a little" hyperbole from time to time (Courtesy of lev radin/ Shutterstock.com). [49]

Lesson Summary

A bit of overstatement at times can be very helpful to the advancement of your career (and undue candor can on occasion hurt), but remember employers have long memories, so it pays never to check your ethical compass at the door – truths stretched too far are ultimately as ineffective as untruths.

Nepos Section on the Conduct of Atticus

(3.1) "Furthermore, his (Atticus) conduct in Athens was such that he showed himself gracious to the humble and on equality with the great."

(3.2) "(The citizens of Athens) found him an advisor and a help in all the administration of their state."

As the biographer of Atticus concludes his description of the settlement of Atticus into his new

2 - The Early Life of Atticus

home in Athens, we next find three examples offered by Nepos as proof of young Atticus' early maturity and wisdom. The first example is that from the time of his arrival in Athens there is an absence of arrogance, for Nepos states that Atticus is "gracious to the humble". This character trait is even more pronounced when you consider that when Atticus arrived he was a Roman aristocrat amongst the recently defeated Athenians. The second instance offered by Nepos is that even as a youth Atticus was not to be intimidated, for he demonstrated "equality with the great". The third and final instance of the wisdom of Atticus is that he became an advisor to the Athenian government in the administration (and perhaps the post-war financial restructuring) of their ravaged city.

Lesson 7: Obsess about Timing

Clearly Atticus had a knack for charming people, but the more critical point here for us is that Atticus wisely seized the opportunity to advise the government of Athens, most likely as a natural furtherance of his financial interests and he did so at a most opportune time – a period following defeat when the people of Athens were most vulnerable and in need of support from influential Romans.

The lesson to be mastered from Atticus' attitude and actions in Athens is the importance of timing. For if Atticus had not seized the opportunity to work with the Athenian officials when he did, or had alienated them through arrogance when support was most needed, Atticus would have lost the chance to befriend the Athenians in their time of greatest need. By acting when the need was most

Career Turbulence

acute Atticus performed a service that would be long remembered and honored by the Athenians.

Theodore Roosevelt, the youngest person in U.S. history to rise to the presidency of the United States and a man who never shied from a tough decision or battle, was well aware of the importance of timing when he admitted, "Nine-tenths of wisdom is being wise in time."[50]

Figure 2.10: President Theodore Roosevelt not only recognized the value of speaking softly and carrying a big stick, he well knew the importance of time management in his decision-making. [51]

Lesson Summary

We frequently fail to consider time as a critical component of our decision process. Often, only when time runs short or an opportunity has passed us by do we realize that the absence of time is our worst enemy, and that we failed to recognize it as such when faced with making a critical decision. Time is

2 - The Early Life of Atticus

a very precious resource, and once wasted, time can never be recovered or restored.

Chapter Review

Let us review once more the important wealth preservation lessons that emerged from studying Atticus' early life and relocation from Rome to Athens during the years of 109 BC to 85 BC. It is important to note that these first seven lessons emerged from the early challenges Atticus faced in his youth. You may decide not to employ any of these lessons in your fight to preserve (or enhance) a career, but they are presented, as are all the lessons in this text, as tools with which you at least should be familiar, especially during periods of crises.

Lesson 1: Self-promotion is no Vice

If you do not sing your own praises it is hard to find a chorus to back you up. But always remember, however, that self-praise must be based upon real and continued success, or it quickly becomes the mere bragging of a blowhard. Therefore a careful balance must be maintained so that self-praise always appears well earned and justified.

Lesson 2: Cultivate the Powerful

A good indicator of your influence is the stature of your friends, but the more lofty the perch of your bedfellows, the more sensitive and susceptible they are to the influence of internal and external politics. So if you are prepared to throw them over in the heat of a crisis, be assured that they are prepared to do the same to you.

Career Turbulence

Lesson 3: Get the hell out of Dodge

Business conflict is like a contact sport, so know when you should be a player and when it is best to be a spectator. Nonalignment and nonparticipation are often thought of as demonstrating weakness of character, so be prepared for the criticism and look to offer counter examples (perhaps elucidated through self-praise) in order to counteract the perception of cowardice or the accusation of being a turncoat – labels to be avoided if at all possible.

Lesson 4: Cash is King

In times of crisis simply keep your assets as liquid as possible and your debts as small as is feasible.

Lesson 5: Firmness is not Synonymous with Abrasiveness

It's better to be the reluctant disciplinarian than the enthusiastic bully, for the instilling of fear is not a long-term strategy for success. Firmness of action, however, is an essential part of a manager's repertoire.

Lesson 6: Do not Dismiss the Value of an Occasional Overstatement

Very often a little embellishment of the truth can be helpful in opening doors and winning friends, but when it comes time to deliver there can be no near misses –you must do all that you committed.

Lesson 7: Obsess about Timing

Timing and time management are crucially important to the deliberative process and even more so during a crisis. The failure to remain exquisitely sensitive to timing will only complicate decisions and reduce options. In any crisis, obsession with time is truly a virtue and not a vice.

Career Turbulence

CHAPTER 3

A Banker in Athens

Timeline for major events in this chapter
(85 BC - 61 BC)

Date (BC)	Major Event	Age of Atticus
82 - 81	Dictatorship of Sulla	27 - 28
65	Atticus Returns to Rome	44
63	Cicero Elected Consul Birth of Octavius	46

Period Background

This period of Atticus' adulthood begins with Sulla's victorious return march through Athens and back to Rome in 83 BC for what would be Sulla's second invasion of his native capital. Sulla would spend time in Athens before embarking upon his bloody campaign of revenge against those who operated against him in Rome. To emphasize what Sulla's victory meant to his enemies (whom Atticus refused to join), we turn to Plutarch, an ancient Roman historian writing more than a century after Nepos. Plutarch wrote:

Career Turbulence

"Sylla (Sulla) gathered together in the circus... six thousand (survivors of the battle against Sulla), and just as he commenced speaking to the senate, in the temple of Bellona, proceeded to cut them down, by men appointed for that service. The cry of so vast a multitude put to the sword, in so narrow a space, was naturally heard some distance, and startled the senators. He, however, continuing his speech with a calm and unconcerned countenance, bade them to listen to what he had to say, and not busy themselves with what was doing outdoors; he had given directions for the chastisement of some offenders."[52]

The intimidated Senators quickly appointed Sulla dictator (a position historically limited to six months) with no limit set to his time in office.

Sulla's Precedent for Obtaining Power

Sulla thus established an unfortunate precedent for the means to obtain power during the last years of the Roman Republic and that example was closely observed by the ambitious younger Roman elites of the day, including the future consuls Pompey the Great and Marcus Crassus, both of whom served under Sulla's command.

3 - A Banker in Athens

Figure 3.1: Shows a marble bust of Pompey the Great. Pompey served under Sulla and Sulla was so impressed by Pompey that he offered his stepdaughter in marriage to the young officer. [53]

Figure 3.2: Shows a marble bust of the Roman Senator Crassus.[54] *Crassus, like Pompey, also served under Sulla and was to become one of the wealthiest Senators in Rome's history.*

Career Turbulence

Sulla and Caesar

Additionally Sulla's ascension would also have been keenly followed by the young Julius Caesar, but in his case, from the perspective of a potential adversary. For Caesar, although still rather young, had family ties to Sulla's enemy, Marius, and therefore his life was in danger (not unlike Atticus' situation a few years earlier, and Caesar also left Rome, but for a brief period only). Sulla was of a mind to have Caesar killed, but was dissuaded by the appeal of some friends: nonetheless, Sulla, who was a very astute judge of men, commented, "... they had no sense if they did not see in this boy (Caesar) many Mariuses." [55]

Figure 3.3: Shows a marble bust of Caesar who had family ties to Marius. Sulla was dissuaded from executing Caesar in his youth, but warned that there were many Mariuses in the boy.[56]

3 - A Banker in Athens

Cicero – the Fourth Rising Star

These three young men coming of age under Sulla would eventually share the leadership of the Roman Republic – or what remained of it politically – amongst them. A fourth rising star to cut his teeth under Sulla's regime was a spindly young lawyer with a nervous stomach and a brilliant mind – Cicero. Cicero was no acolyte of Sulla's and courageously chose to defend an abused victim of one of Sulla's chief henchmen. Cicero won what became a blockbuster of a legal case and clearly established himself as a young man to watch.[57] However, any watching had to be done at a distance, for after winning his case, and embarrassing Sulla; young Cicero, like his friend Atticus and Caesar, removed himself from Rome. Cicero unsurprisingly took up residence in Athens.[58] The reason for Cicero's departure, which was in 79 BC, was ostensibly for medical reasons, but in Athens he could avoid the wrath of Sulla, study, and also enjoy the companionship of his old schoolmate, Atticus.[59]

Figure 3.4: Shows a marble bust of Cicero late in his life.[60] The young Cicero began his rise to fame not on the field of battle, but in the courts, during the dictatorship of Sulla.

Career Turbulence

All Four Major Players find a Path to Glory

So we see that all the major players in the drama of the fall of the Roman Republic were now on their respective paths to fame (Cicero and Caesar are well remembered to this day), wealth (Crassus became the richest man in the history of the Roman Republic), power (the Senate would entrust Pompey with supreme power in an effort to thwart Caesar's rebellious march along Sulla's bloody route) and death (all would die in the cataclysm that was the collapse of the Republic). And among these power brokers Atticus found the means to survive. Atticus' survival, however, was never a sure bet and if we return to the time of Sulla and his stay in Athens, before commencing his second march on Rome (in 83 BC), we find Nepos picking up the story of the soon to be dictator and his fondness for the youthful and engaging Atticus.

Nepos on Atticus and Sulla

(4.1) "When Sulla had come to Athens on his way home from Asia, so long as he remained there he kept Atticus with him."

(4.2) "But when he (Sulla) tried to persuade him (to return to Rome), Atticus answered: "Do not, I pray you, try to lead me against those with whom I refused to bear arms against you but preferred to leave Italy." Whereupon Sulla praised the young man for his sense of duty."

Sulla had been much derided for his love of entertainers such as actors, dancers, musicians, and even jesters, for such "lowlifes" were beneath the dignity of most aristocrats (and ancient Roman

3 - A Banker in Athens

historians) but Sulla reveled and relaxed in their company. Perhaps then it is no surprise that in war ravaged Athens, Sulla, seeking entertainment as a diversion wherever he might find it, would be enchanted with the intellectual Atticus; for Atticus had a great affinity for the arts, spoke and read Greek fluently, and along with his flawless Latin, could recite poetry in either language.

Sulla's Invitation

Sulla was sufficiently taken with Atticus to try and "persuade" Atticus to return to Rome with him. Now this was an extremely dangerous moment for Atticus. We can safely assume Sulla was not a man likely to accept rejection well (Sulla's self-selected epitaph was something akin to there being no better friend or worse enemy than he). In this instance, Atticus presumably displayed great courage, declining Sulla's invitation to join him on his return to Rome and explaining the rationale for his decision by saying: "Do not, I pray you, try to lead me against those with whom I refused to bear arms against you…" Nepos avoids any charge of cowardice on Atticus' part, by directly quoting the statement to demonstrate Atticus' courage and "sense of duty" in the face of Sulla's "request."

Sulla Praises Atticus

Fortunately for Atticus, the result of his decision to reject Sulla's offer was that Sulla reacted with not anger but praise, and we can assume Atticus breathed a deep sigh of relief. The question we must ask is why did Atticus decline at this point in the hostilities. Although not a sure thing, Sulla must

Career Turbulence

have looked to be holding the stronger hand. The assumption we might easily make is that Atticus simply spoke the truth and wished to choose no side at all. However, it is also possible that the true genius of Atticus' decision was to act on an understanding that the wheel of fortune turns slowly, but turn it does, and when Sulla was no longer on the scene memories of the vanquished (including surviving family members of the dead) would linger for generations and those memories most likely offered only additional chaos and bloodshed. Atticus wisely opted for long-term neutrality and not a short-term victory.

Neutrality in Crisis as a Strategy

The critical point here for a modern business person to draw from Atticus' dealing with Sulla is simple but frequently overlooked in the rush to choose a winning side during a crisis, when players are lining up on all sides of the issue at hand. **The key is to remember that it is not always necessary to choose a winner or winning side. However, the choice to remain neutral is very difficult, because typically each side will claim the moral high ground and, worse still, apply the biblical admonition of Jesus, "Whoever is not with Me is against Me."** [61]

Lesson 8: Consider Neutrality as an Option in a Political Conflict.

In the case of Atticus and Sulla, Atticus courageously managed to avoid choosing a side, and ultimately benefited by alienating neither faction in the process. However, since an unaligned approach to a looming crisis is so often not well received by the major participants, it is important to be prepared for abuse as a result of your neutrality. President John F. Kennedy at the height of the Cold War condemned those who failed to choose his side in a moral crisis with a quote from Dante's Inferno. Kennedy stated, "Dante once said that the hottest places in hell are reserved for those who in a period of moral crisis maintain their neutrality."[62]

Figure 3.5: President John F. Kennedy in 1963 reminded a German audience, and the world that hell awaited those who sought neutrality in a moral crisis.[63]

Lesson Summary

Neutrality as a strategy is simple in theory and exquisitely difficult in practice. Do not allow the abuse you suffer if you choose this course to deflect you from your position. This lesson is not intended as an argument for always choosing a neutral position in a conflict, but rather the consideration of neutrality as an additional option before choosing

Career Turbulence

sides. Typically success depends on choosing the right side, and sometimes the right side can be no side at all; however such a choice will, as described earlier, often come with significant baggage.

Nepos on Friends of Atticus

(4.3) "Atticus gave to his property as much attention as was the duty of a careful head of a family."

(4.4) "At the same time he rendered service to his friends at Rome; for he always appeared on the occasion of their candidacy for office, and was at hand whenever any important action was taken. Thus to Cicero in all his times of peril he showed unparalleled loyalty, and when the orator was on his way to exile, he made him a present of two hundred and fifty thousand sesterces."

Here we now see the myth making of Nepos in full swing. Atticus is presented not as the hardworking businessman but rather the devoted family man who only gave his business interests as much time as was his "duty". In reality we know that Atticus was very focused on his business enterprises, to an extent that perhaps he wished not to be well known, since being too devoted to business in ancient Rome was looked upon as something unseemly and crass. We, however, know how preoccupied Atticus was with his business interests because of a letter from Cicero to Atticus in January of 60 BC, when Cicero was desperate to have Atticus in Rome. Cicero wrote asking to his friend to return for a census, and reminded Atticus, a bit tongue in cheek, that registration "... at the very end of the census period is a real businessman's style."[64] This was a lighthearted joke between friends, but indicative indeed of the time Atticus was spending on his growing business empire.

Atticus' Network of Associates

The other point made in section 4.4 above about Atticus' "service to his friends at Rome" requires a bit more exploration as well. Nepos would have his readers believe that Atticus' commitment, as described here, is nothing more than a further demonstration of his altruistic nature.

Nepos is certainly correct to point out the loyalty displayed by Atticus in travelling from Athens to Rome in support of his friends' candidacies and "important actions". However, we should examine the possibility for other motives of Atticus, beyond Nepos' assertion of "duty" and "loyalty" and ask if there are additional benefits that would accrue to Atticus from a frequent presence in Rome during the period of the 80s–60s BC? The answer, from a business perspective, is clearly yes. There are a number of reasons as to why Atticus would have wanted to make return visits to Rome with some regularity and staying for sufficient durations in Rome. Those reasons include:

1. To learn first hand about important events
2. To visit his existing clients
3. To solicit new clients
4. To strengthen political ties with influential Senators
5. To ensure that connections with other equestrians and bankers remained active and strong.

Career Turbulence

As Atticus' business empire grew, he would certainly have recognized the importance of staying close to his clients, financial associates (e.g. other equestrians as well as other bankers), senators, and his intimate friends.

Lesson 9: It's Who you Know that Makes the Difference

The care and feeding of your network of friends (and not just those in high places) is a critical element of any businessperson's success. The term used today is "networking", and no businessperson can long succeed without doing so. Atticus clearly put in practice the old adage that it is "… who you know that makes the difference."[65]

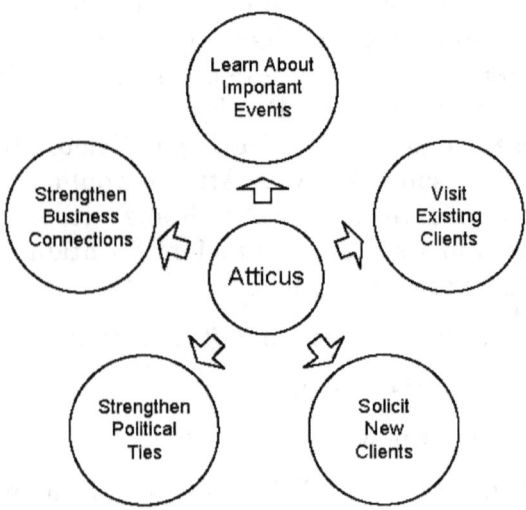

Figure 3.6: Shows Atticus carefully tended his network of contacts and offers a rationale beyond displaying loyalty to friends for Atticus' not infrequent visits to Rome. Atticus clearly put in practice the old adage that it is who you know that is important.

3 - A Banker in Athens

At the center of anyone's network of contacts should be the core of close friends and allies from whom trust and reliance can be readily assumed. However, it is also important to remember that the further one moves from that core group of loyalists the more care must be taken to ensure that the reliability of an associate can safely be assured -- especially in a crisis.

Lesson Summary

An employee in any organization, regardless of its size, would do well to emulate Atticus in his efforts to create and sustain his network of associates. Those efforts should be targeted not just inside the company in which you are employed but also outside the organization in order to ensure that your support network does not become crippled due to the threatened loss of a job. The four key elements of network development most likely employed by Atticus, and certainly necessary to develop and enlarge your network, include:

1. Stay in frequent contact with existing network members
2. Target and woo new members into your network.
3. Listen to the information and advice that emerges from your network.
4. Invest time and energy in your network's maintenance.

These four elements are summarized Figure 3.7 below.

Career Turbulence

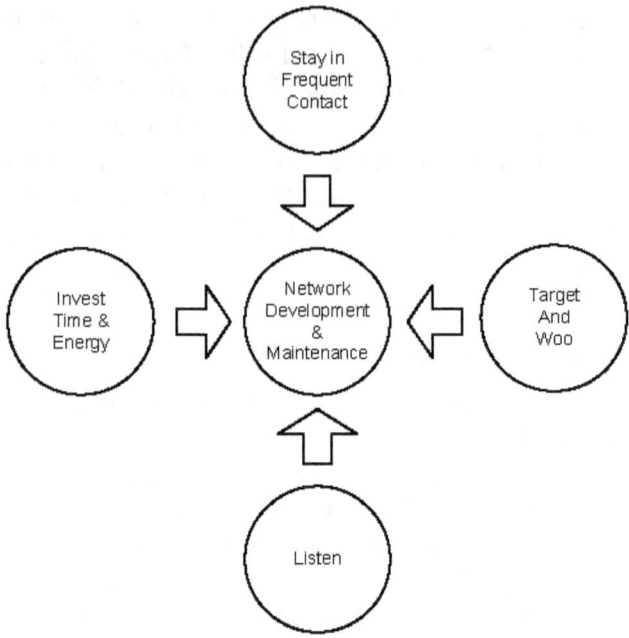

Figure 3.7: This Figure depicts the key elements of network development and maintenance.

Atticus' Gift to Cicero

Nepos likely inserted the reference about the financial support of Cicero in exile as a further re-enforcement of his proof that Atticus was a loyal, in fact a very loyal friend, since he supported his friend, Cicero, in the period of Cicero's expulsion from Rome and did so with a significant financial "present" of 250,000 sesterces (approximately $1M). A few points should be noted here with regard to this transaction since Nepos said nothing more of it or Cicero's exile and eventual return. First, this episode occurred in 58 BC, five years after Cicero had been elected and served as consul of Rome.

Second, by that time Atticus was resident in Rome, and his support of Cicero was based on Atticus' understanding of the political maneuvering among Caesar, Pompey, Crassus and the rest of the Senate. Cicero was a merely pawn caught between more powerful competing interests, with the result that Cicero was banished from Rome for over a year – a clear demonstration of the risks Senators, even those of Cicero's consular status, would potentially face if they angered Caesar, Pompey or Crassus (who at the time were political allies).

Cicero Casts Blame for his Exile

Nepos may simply have desired to make the point that in a well-known case of exile, Atticus remained steadfast in his friendship with the disgraced Cicero and the amount of the financial gift supports that interpretation. However, Professor Welch argues that careful study of Cicero's letters from this period hints that there was more to the story.[66] Welch points to Atticus himself as being blamed, at least in part, by Cicero for his exile! Two of Cicero's letters, one to his brother, Quintus, and a second written to Atticus are key to Welch's incrimination of Atticus.

In the letter to his brother, Cicero (while still in exile) wrote, "My own fault lay in trusting men in whom I thought it would be an abomination to deceive me or even imagined that it was not in their interest to do so."[67] Cicero felt his friends then played a role, but Atticus too?

The letter to Atticus was written after Cicero's return from exile. In it Welch notes that Cicero may have forgiven Atticus but not forgotten, for Cicero wrote, "I had found you, to be quite frank, neither bolder nor wiser than myself as an advisor, nor may I add, excessively sedulous in guarding me from harm."[68] This condemnation may be a bit tangential, but is still biting, given that the criticism was made in a letter written upon Cicero's joyous return to Rome just after the Senate nullified his exile in September 57 BC.

So we have Atticus being praised by his biographer Nepos for his generous support of Cicero, his friend, banking client, and brother-in-law of Atticus' sister (Cicero's brother Quintus was married to Atticus' sister). Alternatively Cicero is complaining to Atticus that Atticus was too passive in his efforts to prevent Cicero from being exiled. Clearly Atticus did provide Cicero with a substantial gift, but was it pure generosity or was it generosity prodded by a guilty conscience?

The Motivation of Atticus

What possibly could have motivated Atticus to have done as implied by Cicero? There must have been an extraordinary reason for Atticus to jeopardize the career and possibly even the life of his good friend. Cicero himself provides the answer in that same letter written to his brother, stating two reasons for the action of his friends – that his friends were either jealous of him (typical Cicero and certainly unlikely for Atticus) or more importantly, they were "afraid for themselves."[69] So here we have what is most likely the truth. Cicero's friends, possibly including Atticus, chose self-preservation over the risk of attempting to protect Cicero from the onslaught of his very powerful political adversaries. Cicero, though angry, — and we can assume hurt as well, — was forgiving of Atticus, as evidenced by the subsequent flood of letters between the old friends. Cicero must have understood that there were limits to how far he could expect his friends, — even his dear Atticus, — to go in protecting his interests, for at the time of his exile, Cicero too was desperately struggling to find a way to preserve both his life and his dignity. The point for us to recognize is that the constancy of Atticus' loyalty was tested, and when ultimately placed in competition with his instinct for self-preservation, we see that self-preservation won.

Lesson 10: Self-Preservation Trumps Trust

From our examination of the relationship of Atticus and Cicero under extreme stress we can take away the very important business lesson (see Figure 3.8 below) that loyalty should never be taken for granted, and the more trying the challenges the greater the possibility that trust will shatter on the shoals of self-preservation of either career or personal wealth.

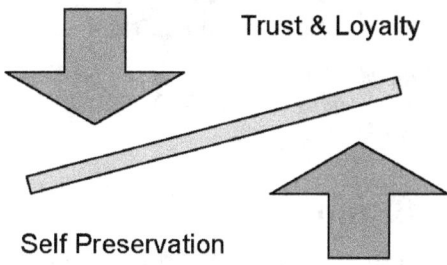

Figure 3.8: During periods of great stress (e.g. a company's downsizing) the historical balance between trust/loyalty and the preservation of one's career can be upended and so must be frequently re-evaluated to ensure traditional emotions are not impeding one's choosing the correct course for career survival and wealth preservation.

Career Turbulence

The balance seen in Figure 3.8 above is perhaps most explicitly and brutally expressed in a famous line from the movie *The Godfather,* when the Godfather's son, Sonny Corleone, is advised that, "Even shooting your father was business not personal, Sonny!"[70]

Figure 3.9: Shows a 1972 poster from the movie The Godfather (Photo by: Mary Evans/PARAMOUNT PICTURES/Ronald Grant/Everett Collection). [71]

Lesson Summary

The Godfather certainly offered the best of Hollywood theatrics, but the point is one that has been made often: when business overlaps the personal, do not ever assume or expect loyalty to preclude self-interest. As Atticus demonstrated, one cannot get too sentimental if it will impede following the correct course or making the difficult decision.

3 - A Banker in Athens

Nepos on Atticus' Return to Rome
(4.5) "After calm had been established in Rome he returned to the city (in 65 BC when his schoolmate Torquatus became consul and two years in advance of Cicero becoming consul)."

Even after Sulla's death in 78 BC Atticus chose to remain in Athens. It was not until 65 BC that Atticus relocated back to Rome. By that year Atticus' closest friends were beginning to manage the government of Rome (Torquatus was elected consul for 65 BC and Cicero for 63 BC). It should also be noted that a consul's influence did not vanish after leaving office and so provided a former consul the opportunity for significant power in the Senate as well as in the future administration of the Roman Republic. Therefore if Atticus needed assistance he would have had very powerful allies in his former childhood schoolmates. What better time could there be for a businessman to return to Rome than when his intimates controlled the ship of state?

The Reach of Atticus
There is an interesting example of Atticus' attempt to benefit from these powerful relationships in his efforts to collect on a loan he made to the ancient Greek city of Sicyon. Cicero was so well aware of (and used to) Atticus' persistent efforts to obtain repayment of the loan that he jokingly referred to those efforts in 61 BC as "the siege of Sicyon."[72] With regard to this same debt in 60 BC Cicero wrote, "You often write me about your affair, in which I can do nothing to help. ... If you still manage to coax a sesterce or two out of the Sicyonians I shall be glad

Career Turbulence

to hear of it."[73] Atticus was a determined banker when it came to collecting his debts and despite Cicero's inability to assist in the matter there were still more references to Sicyon in Cicero's letters as late as 59 BC. Then, interestingly, the subject of the loan collection after that date is dropped.

Did Atticus give up on collecting the debt? We do not know. However, it is intriguing that nearly a century later, the ancient author and encyclopedist Pliny the Elder wrote of Sicyon that it:

> "...was for a long period a native place of painting. But all the pictures there had been sold to meet a debt of the community, and were removed from ownership of the state to Rome..." [74]

There is no mention by Pliny the Elder of who was owed the debt, but Pliny the Elder does provide a date when the debt was settled - 56 BC! Perhaps Atticus (a great lover of art) finally found the means to collect on the loan owed by the Sicyonians, possibly via the intervention of someone even more powerful than Cicero (e.g. one of the triumvirs), but in the absence of any additional information, such speculation must unfortunately remain just that – mere speculation.

Lesson 11: Do not Underestimate the Power of Tenacity

Earlier, when discussing section 1.3-4 above, we reviewed the importance of having friends in high places. The lesson from this section is not the re-iteration of the importance of powerful associates,

3 - A Banker in Athens

but rather how essential determination and focus are to any task. Atticus spent years working on the collection of this loan and seemed to have pushed the issue almost beyond even Cicero's tolerance. **Atticus' demonstrated that tenacity, even if in failure, still remains an excellent model for today's business environments with its accelerated event horizons. Technology may have conditioned us expect to instantaneous responses but not all problems lend themselves to rapid resolution. Tenacity must remain a critical component of your problem solving efforts.**

Looking again to Napoleon Bonaparte for insight into the importance of perseverance in a successful career, we find that he declared that, "The truest wisdom is a resolute determination."[75] Napoleon's successful climb to the pinnacle of power in France demonstrated the benefit, and the importance, of resolute determination. However, Napoleon, by pushing too far and too hard into the territory where absolute determination gives way to stubbornness and arrogance, also demonstrated that there is a limit to every rule. Perhaps Atticus, too, as indicated by Cicero's comments about Atticus' "siege of Sicyon" was approaching just that point in his determined efforts to collect the debt of the Sicyonians, but the fact remains that tenacity is an essential component of one's success not just in long term but in the short term as well.

Career Turbulence

Figure 3.10: Napoleon Bonaparte acted with resolute determination but pushed the point beyond the extreme and as a result was ultimately defeated and exiled. Here, as painted by Adolf Northen, we see a depiction of Napoleon's retreat from Russia in the winter of 1812.[76]

Lesson Summary

Resolute determination is a core element of both survival and success, but by pressing too hard, a career can be just as jeopardized, as it might be due to the absence of tenacity. Napoleon was ultimately defeated and exiled, but the importance of the basic point remains. Success is never guaranteed, but failure surely will be if the job at hand is not attacked with sufficient tenacity. Atticus' surely demonstrated such tenacity in his efforts to collect the debt owed him by the Sicyonians but whether he was truly successful or not is unfortunately lost in the dark recesses of history.

3 - A Banker in Athens

Chapter Review

As power in the Republic passed from one generation to the next, we saw that Atticus carefully managed his relationships with the current and emerging powerful political stakeholders of the Roman Republic (See Figure 3.10 below).

Stakeholder Infuence	85 BC - 81 BC	80 BC - 61 BC
Significant (e.g. Keep Satisfied)	Sulla Marius	Pompey Crassus Cicero
Moderate (e.g. Keep Informed)	Cicero	Caesar
Little or None (e.g. Keep in Contact)	Caesar Pompey Crassus	Antony Brutus

Figure 3.11: A stakeholder matrix of Atticus' possible relationships with key and emerging political players while he was still just a young adult.

The key job preservation lessons formed from the study of Atticus' actions during the Roman Republic's violent and unsettled period during the years following Sulla's rise and dictatorship are:

Lesson 8: Consider Neutrality as an Option in a Political Conflict

Always consider neutrality as an option in a conflict, but again be prepared for abuse if neutrality is your chosen course, because in any political battle participants are always thinking if you are not with me you are against me.

Lesson 9: It's Who you Know that Makes the Difference

Network, network and network some more.

Lesson 10: Self-Preservation Trumps Trust

The greater the crisis the more difficult the decisions, and the more necessary it is to strip away the vestiges of emotion that inhibit a dispassionate analysis of the options and their risks. This is not an argument to remove the passion from the person but to remove the person from the passion.

Lesson 11: Do not Underestimate the Power of Tenacity

To see a difficult and complex task through to its ultimate completion is an essential operating principle for any businessperson, and always remember that being meticulous in attention to the mundane is no flaw. However, undue concentration on the details will obscure the larger picture; so make sure the small stuff is covered without defocusing from the strategic issues at hand.

CHAPTER 4

Wealth Preservation in Rome

Timeline for Major Events in this Chapter (60 BC - 45 BC)

Date (BC)	Major Event	Age of Atticus
60	Republic Led by Caesar, Pompey and Crassus (Called the First Triumvirate)	49
58	Cicero Exiled Atticus Inherits 10M Sesterces from Caecilius	51
57	Cicero's Return from Exile	52
56	Atticus Marries Pilia	53
54	Death of Julia, Caesar's Daughter, Pompey's Wife	55
53	Crassus Killed in Parthia	56
49	Caesar's Civil War Begins	60
48	Caesar's Defeat of Pompey Dictatorship of Caesar Begins	61
47	Caesar Pardons Cicero for Supporting Pompey	62

Career Turbulence

Period Background

The young Pompey, Crassus, and Caesar had begun their careers under Sulla's long shadow, and by 60 BC the three were well positioned and ready to make their move; they combined their efforts and seized control of the machinery of the Republic. The alliance they formed is known to history as the First Triumvirate; though the alliance had no official status within the Roman Republic. The three men (with Caesar initially as the junior member) had such influence that they effectively controlled the Senate, government appointees, and the military. We saw earlier that even Cicero, a former Roman consul and one of the most famous men of his day, could be treated as a criminal and exiled with little difficulty (his houses in Rome were also burned to the ground). Power sharing however, has it challenges, and two key events destabilized the equilibrium of the Triumvirs. Pompey had been married to Caesar's daughter (Julia) until her death during childbirth in 54 BC. Pompey keenly felt Julia's death and the relationship between Pompey and Caesar suffered from her loss. The death of Crassus, who was killed in an ill-advised military expedition in 53 BC, completed the destabilization process with the result that Pompey and Caesar fell out.

The result was that the Senate had perhaps its final opportunity to assert itself and restore the integrity of the Republic. An effort to contain Caesar was led by a faction of conservative senators (the Optimates) and they worked to draw Pompey into their camp and demonize Caesar. The result was not the peaceable restoration of the Republic, but rather the antagonizing of Caesar, a popular politician and victorious general with tens of thousands of battle-hardened and loyal legionnaires at his back. Pompey accepted a grant of supreme power by the Senate in 52 BC and so as the decade of the fifties ended, the two most powerful men in Rome, former allies and relations by marriage prepared to face off for control of the Roman world.

Caesar Crosses the Rubicon

Given the Senate's belated and misguided actions, Caesar chose to cross the Rubicon with his legions and advance on Rome (like Sulla before him). The Rubicon is a river in northern Italy that served as an ancient boundary that could not be crossed by a magistrate with his troops. Therefore when Caesar moved his troops across the small river, he signaled that he had decided war was his only viable option to preserve his dignity and his life. Civil war ensued. The outcome of this second civil war in the lifetime of Atticus was Caesar's complete defeat of the senatorial forces by 48 BC and the death of Pompey. The Roman Republic again was under the heel of a victorious general and a cowered Senate named Caesar Dictator. During this time of conflict, as "the dogs of war"[77] escaped from their frayed harnesses, we will see that Atticus and Cicero took divergent paths with the result that Atticus succeeded in protecting his life, family and wealth, while Cicero did not.

Career Turbulence

Nepos on Atticus Inherits Again

(5.1) "His (Atticus') maternal uncle was Quintus Caecilius, a Roman knight,[78] ... rich but very hard to please. Atticus treated the sour-tempered old man with such deference, that although no one else could endure him, his nephew retained his good-will without giving him any offence until he reached extreme old age. By such conduct he (Atticus) reaped the fruits of his devotion;"

(5.2) "for Caecilius, on his deathbed adopted him by will and made him heir to three-fourths of his estate; and his share came to about ten million sestertii."[79]

We now have yet another reason why Atticus may have frequently returned to Rome from Athens: devotion to his fabulously wealthy uncle. An interesting story was circulating in antiquity and memorialized in the first quarter century AD by the Roman historian Valerius Maximus. Maximus wrote that Atticus' uncle:

> "Caecilius had attained a respectable status and ample wealth by the ready patronage and unstinted generosity of L. Lucullus (a powerful lieutenant of Sulla). He (Atticus' uncle) had always given out that Lucullus was his sole heir and on his deathbed gave him his signet rings. In his will however, he adopted Pomponius Atticus and left him heir to all he possessed. But the Roman people put a rope round the neck of the treacherous deceiver and dragged his corpse through the streets. So the villain had the son and heir he wanted (Atticus), but funeral obsequies such as he deserved." [80]

Cicero's Comments on the Caecilius Affair

We should note however, that as juicy as this tale is, when Atticus came into his inheritance in 58 BC Cicero wrote to Atticus and merely said, "Well I heartily approve that it is so and that your uncle has done the proper thing."[81] There was no mention by Cicero of the corpse of Atticus' uncle being dragged through the streets of Rome. Regardless of whether there is any historical truth to the gruesome event, one very important fact emerged from the story. The inheritance of 10 million sesterces dramatically increased the wealth and the influence of Atticus just as the structure of the Roman Republic was undergoing its final stages of instability.

Nepos' Portrayal of Atticus' Devotion

One could simply say here that Atticus was just plain lucky to find himself with such a windfall. However, that would be naïve because we know from the text of Nepos that Atticus demonstrated great forbearance with his difficult uncle while others did not. From Maximus' description of Caecilius' deathbed double-cross of his assumed heir Lucullus, a loyal friend and patron of his career, we obtain a glimpse of the character of the man Atticus endured. The inheritance by Atticus could not have been a sure thing, but Nepos would have us believe that Atticus' devotion to his dying uncle was merely another example of Atticus' magnanimity and that the size of the potential inheritance was irrelevant to Atticus' exemplary example of filial devotion.

Career Turbulence

Lesson 12: Skepticism is a Virtue

The lesson from this example of Atticus is to think before taking someone (be it Nepos, your boss, a business associate, a friend, or even a dying relative) completely at face value. This cautious approach to dealing with others, especially in times of great stress, was well articulated by J. Pierpont Morgan, perhaps the best-known and most powerful banker in American history. Morgan advised, "A man generally has two reasons for doing a thing. One that sounds good, and a real one."[82]

Figure 4.1: Shows J. P. Morgan perhaps America's greatest banker.[83] Morgan and his banking institution helped in the formation of General Electric and United States Steel Corporation. Today JPMorgan Chase & Company has assets of $2.3 Trillion dollars. [84]

4 - Wealth Preservation in Rome

Lesson Summary

As J.P. Morgan advised, always be a skeptic and look beyond the surface to help ensure that you understand the motivations of the individual with whom you are dealing. In turbulent times (as well as in "good times") it is very risky to take individuals at face value and it is best to look long and hard at motivations in order to avoid unpleasant surprises.

Atticus' Lifestyle

Despite Atticus' greatly enhanced financial position he continued to live a relatively frugal lifestyle that drew positive comments from both Cicero and Nepos (See Appendix D for more details on Atticus' lifestyle). Atticus wisely shunned ostentatious displays of wealth that might give rise to envy by the more powerful. It was most likely the size of this inheritance that allowed Atticus the opportunity to fund that generous donation of grain to the people of Athens in 55 BC (three years after the death of Atticus' wealthy uncle) that we discussed earlier in the text. Additionally, a couple of years following the receipt of his 10 million sesterces inheritance, Atticus, at the age of 53, married a young woman named Pilia,[85] (we know the timeframe from a letter of Cicero who had attended the wedding).[86] Atticus and Pilia had one daughter (whose betrothal we will discuss later in the text) and remained married for 12 years until Pilia's death in 44 BC.

Career Turbulence

Nepos on Atticus and the Optimates

(6.1) "In public life he (Atticus) so conducted himself as always to be, and to be regarded as being, on the side of the best men, yet he did not trust himself to the waves of civil strife."

Here we find Nepos providing a rare glimpse into the political positioning of Atticus. We first are informed that Atticus "so conducted himself as always to be, and to be regarded as being, on the side of the best men." This perhaps is our clearest indication from Nepos (along with an occasional mention of Atticus' banking clients) that Atticus was on the side of the Optimates. This is not a total surprise, for as a banker Atticus would typically be supportive of the faction most likely to retain the status quo, which would have included a policy in favor of keeping interest rates at current levels (preferably high) and against any efforts to cancel debts (at times a platform of the Populares).

Atticus' businesslike attitude to politics is not surprising, and Cicero on occasion even attempted to emulate his friend's approach, for we see in 55 BC (two years after his return from exile) that Cicero wrote Atticus in what must have been a response to a plea by Atticus for him to be more careful. Cicero wrote, "As for your admonition to behave like a politique,[87] and to keep to the inner row (a place of safety in an ancient board game), I shall do so."[88]

The Caution of Atticus

Nepos also tells us that Atticus "did not trust himself to the waves of civil strife." Here again we see the caution of Atticus. We saw that Atticus while still a young man chose flight to Athens as a means to avoid choosing sides during the civil unrest of Sulla's time. Thirty years later there is again a period of great unrest and although flight is not chosen by Atticus, Nepos strongly hints that despite Atticus' support for the Optimates, he did not publicly choose their side. We should note that the absence of public support does not mean that Atticus did not choose to provide support quietly, behind the scenes, in a way that would have no visibility to the public (or the powerful) and perhaps even to his biographer. This possibility must be considered because of what we next learn from Cicero about Atticus' outlook at this time.

Atticus the "Political Animal"

Cicero, in a letter to Atticus in 55 BC, both reaffirmed the correctness of Nepos' description of Atticus' ability to avoid the public tumult and laments his own inability to maintain "the inner row." Cicero writes:

> "for you, though you are a political animal bynature, are not subject to any peculiar servitude... But for me, reckoned a madman if I speak on politics as I ought, a slave if I say what is expedient, and a helpless captive if I say nothing... I must join the fray." [89]

Career Turbulence

This brief description of Atticus by Cicero is extremely critical to the fleshing out Nepos' sparse depiction of Atticus on this most sensitive of subjects – politics.[90] Additionally Cicero provides us a unique insight into his perception of his own political predicament.

We see that Cicero is unequivocal is his acknowledgement that Atticus is political in nature (remember neutral need not mean apolitical). Next Cicero provides us an explanation of how Atticus can manage to remain unaligned – it is because Atticus is free of political servitude. In other words, Atticus owes no one his political support for he is in the debt of none of the major power brokers. Caesar and Pompey may have desired and even demanded Atticus' outright support but Atticus was not obligated to give it. The tremendous wealth of Atticus gave him a freedom of action that few other equestrians could match, although despite his great wealth, he too could still be subject to the intimidation and physical threats that always remained an option to be employed against his desire to remain neutral.

The Constraints on Cicero

Cicero, on the other hand, had spent a lifetime in the public arena and as a result incurred political and financial debts to both Pompey and Caesar – hence his "peculiar servitude." An excellent example of both Cicero's "servitude" and the effectiveness of Atticus' network can be seen in a letter to Atticus from Cicero written in 51 BC in which he instructs Atticus to settle an outstanding loan that Cicero had from Caesar. Cicero wrote, "About Oppius (an

4 - Wealth Preservation in Rome

intimate of Caesar's), you did well to explain to him with regard to the 800,000 (sesterces); ... just get it settled..."[91] Cicero was in substantial financial debt to Caesar and so his freedom of action was severely constrained. Of course his chosen means to resolve this particular constraint was Atticus, who, despite his supposed preference for the Optimates, had surprisingly close ties to Caesar's advisors and was able to resolve a thorny issue for Cicero.

An additional result that emerges from Atticus' determination to stay out of direct involvement in the tumult of the day is that Atticus could remain useful to both sides, even if he was not totally disinterested in the outcome or the winner. That lesson has a very modern component and today is called "realpolitik," which the Merriam-Webster dictionary defines as "politics based on practical and material factors rather than on theoretical or ethical objectives."[92]

We see that when necessary Atticus could ignore his personal predilections in order to achieve the ends he desired – in this case his survival. Atticus was clearly no Cicero, and so the ends in this matter (greater concern for personal well being over the Republic's survival) trumped the means (potentially the abandonment of ones political allies).

Lesson 13: Keep your Passions in Check

The intent of this lesson is to remind the businessperson that it is imperative to keep your passions in check and make decisions based on the logic of the situation and not the emotion of the moment. Benjamin Franklin, an American Founding Father who like Atticus survived the trauma of war, recognized that action driven by unchecked passion was risky and ill advised. It is Franklin, who among his varied interests was also, like Atticus, an author and publisher that counseled, "If passion drives you, let reason hold the reins."[93]

Figure 4.2: Shows a marble bust of Benjamin Franklin sculpted by Jean-Antoine Houdon in 1778.[94] Franklin, like Atticus, was an author, publisher and war survivor.

Lesson Summary

This advice remains as important today as in Franklin's or Atticus' time: passion energizes but must be monitored and guided, for if left uncontrolled, disaster can quickly follow. The converse of this lesson also requires attention. Any businessperson, especially when operating in crisis mode for an extended period of time, runs the risk that his or her passion may eventually wane and the absence of passion can be as dangerous as its overabundance.

4 - Wealth Preservation in Rome

Nepos on Atticus and Pompey

(7.1) "Caesar's civil war broke out when Atticus was about sixty years old. He took advantage of the exemption due to his years and did not stir from the city. (Atticus) ... escaped giving offence to Pompey himself."

(7.2) "He (Atticus) had no emolument at his friend's hands (Pompey's), as the rest had who through him had gained either offices or riches."

Atticus, again, for the second time in his life faced civil war. In his youth he found neutrality and safety by escaping to Athens. Now as a 60 year-old man he chose the same pattern of neutrality but perhaps because of his age (or the recognition that in this coming war there would be no safe havens) stayed in Rome. One might surmise (based on Nepos' scant comments on the temper of the times) that Atticus had confidence in his decision to attempt to ride out the storm in Rome, where we can assume he would have had the greatest opportunity to influence events. However, we again learn from Cicero's letters that Atticus had less than complete confidence in his decision to stay put and remain unaligned.

Cicero's Dilemma

In a letter from October of 50 BC, Cicero demands assistance from Atticus to help him choose a course of action as war looms on the horizon:

"For mercy sake, put all you affection, lavished on me as it is, and all your wisdom, remarkable in every field as I do assure you I regard it,

103

into a single concern, the consideration of my position ..." [95]

Less than six months later, in March of 49 BC, Cicero complains that that Atticus' advice is far from concise when he chastises Atticus, "How completely you cover the ground in giving your advice!"[96] During the buildup to war, Atticus most likely advocated a variety of options to Cicero but we cannot be certain since we lack the letters of Atticus to Cicero.

The Non-Alignment of Atticus

Perhaps Atticus' uncertainty in his advice to Cicero was a reflection of his own lack of confidence in identifying the safest course of action. However, by April 49 BC we find that Atticus formulated and adopted his plan of staying put (which Nepos simply attributes to the privilege of old age), for Cicero grudgingly commented in his letter, "(I) ... approve of this fence sitting of yours, and I look upon your position as different from mine."[97] Although it is possible that Atticus was non-aligned from the start, it is more likely that his position evolved over a period of months as seen in Cicero's letters.

Perhaps as events unfolded, Atticus gained a better understanding of the issues and his options, affording him the confidence to finally decide on a course of action or in this case inaction — fence sitting. It is important to note that Cicero's Latin phrasing (tergiversatio), which is translated by Shackleton Bailey as fence sitting, literally means "the action of turning your back on a task or challenge."[98] Clearly Cicero's approval of Atticus' fence sitting was reluctantly given at best.

4 - Wealth Preservation in Rome

The Risk to Atticus of Neutrality

Nepos also informs us that Atticus' action in no way bothered his "friend" Pompey. This is a somewhat startling revelation because:

1. Nearly five years earlier Cicero had written to Atticus that, "(Pompey) ... spoke appreciatively of your undertaking to arrange his art collection."[99] This was in reference to Atticus' assistance to Pompey in the decoration of the magnificent new theater that Pompey built for the people of Rome. Clearly Atticus' network of powerful friends included Pompey himself.

2. Powerful friends expect loyalty – given Atticus' association with Pompey, it is difficult to believe that Pompey took no offence at Atticus' neutrality. Granted, Atticus may have owed Pompey nothing, but since a relationship existed, Atticus' refusal to offer any support to Pompey must have left other Optimates, if not Pompey himself, questioning his motives.

3. As Caesar approached Rome, Pompey chose to exit the city and "(Pompey) ... issued an edict declaring a state of anarchy, and forsook the city, commanding the Senate to follow (him), and forbidding anyone to remain who preferred country and freedom to tyranny."[100]

Given Atticus' decision to stay in Rome, it is difficult to see his non-aligned status as being completely inoffensive to Pompey. One can assume that at a minimum, if Pompey had emerged victorious,

Career Turbulence

Atticus' friendship with Pompey would have been at risk, and conceivably, even his very survival might have been in jeopardy as well.

Atticus is Judicious in Selecting his Course

Given Atticus' varying advice to Cicero over a period of months we can assume that the military situation between Pompey and Caesar was fluid and that Atticus watched the course of events, fully evaluated his options, and only when a decision was finally required, chose his course. That Atticus, despite the rush of events, took his time in reaching a decision was a critical element in his surviving this crisis – this was not procrastination, but rather the avoidance of jumping to a conclusion prematurely.

Atticus' approach illustrates that a decision may best be made when the maximum amount of information is available, as long as the decision point is still viable. In other words, Atticus most likely delayed making his decision until he felt he could wait no longer. As we discussed earlier it is important to remember the importance of timing, but you should not rush a decision if you have the luxury of time (provided that you use that time wisely). If time is not your ally then do not hesitate to make a decision based on the best available information, for if you pass beyond the point at which a decision must be made or is due, you have erred by waiting too long.

4 - Wealth Preservation in Rome

Balancing Time and the Need for Information

The difficult balance (depicted in Figure 4.3) between the need for more information and the requirement to expeditiously choose a course bedevils the crisis manager and reinforces our earlier lesson (Lesson 7) with regard to the necessity of vigilance as to the role of time in any decision making process.

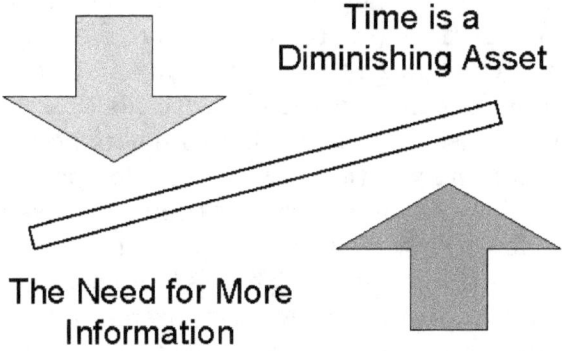

Figure 4.3: Shows the delicate balancing act required in a crisis when choosing between delaying a decision in hopes of obtaining additional information and the risks that that delay may entail.

Neutrality of Atticus Tilts towards Caesar

Atticus decided to distance himself from Pompey as well as the Optimates and assumed a neutral position, again demonstrating his recognition of the fact that in a crisis self-preservation must eclipse loyalty. In early April of 49 BC, a few weeks before Cicero wrote of his grudging acceptance of Atticus' fence sitting, Cicero noted that he had heard that Atticus had "been seen in the Palace." The "Palace" referred to by Cicero was Caesar's home in his

Career Turbulence

capacity as Chief Priest for the Romans and was once a palace for the early kings of Rome. Cicero's distaste for Caesar's monarchial tendencies is clearly evident in this reference to the residence's early use.

Atticus is Less than Forthright with Cicero

Since Atticus was not Cicero's source of information about his visit to Caesar we can infer from Cicero's letter that Atticus had not bothered to discuss his visit in advance with Cicero. Perhaps Atticus was being a bit less than forthright with his close friend Cicero, because Cicero was disinclined to accept any migration by Atticus away from Pompey. That grudging letter from Cicero to Atticus, discussing Atticus' fence sitting, was still weeks away, and so at the time of his visit to Caesar's "Palace," Atticus must have known Cicero was not prepared to accept a shift in Caesar's direction, hence the silence.

Lesson 14: The Deferral of Difficult Decisions Courts Disaster

In this instance, again, we must presume that Atticus' greatest loyalty was not to Cicero but to himself and to his self-preservation. The lesson to be drawn from Atticus' action in this situation is critical, and therefore warrants the reinforcement of one of the greatest orators of the modern era, Winston Churchill. Churchill said, in a 1935 speech to the British House of Commons, as war with Germany loomed on the horizon, "Want of foresight, unwillingness to act when action would be simple and effective, lack of clear thinking, confusion

4 - Wealth Preservation in Rome

of counsel until the emergency comes, until self-preservation strikes its jarring gong - these are the features which constitute the endless repetition of history."[102]

Figure 4.4: Shows a 1940 photograph of Winston Churchill shortly after becoming Prime Minister of Great Britain. Churchill warned his nation very early on as to the threat of Nazi Germany and ultimately led Great Britain to victory in World War II.[103] Churchill, like Atticus, was also an author of history (Churchill won the 1953 Noble Prize in Literature).[104]

Lesson Summary

Churchill, of course, was speaking of Great Britain's failure to act as Adolph Hitler and Nazism reared their ugly visage in Germany and threatened all of Europe. Atticus, on the other hand, was pursuing a much more selfish worldview than that of Churchill; in fact Atticus' chosen course was the antithesis of Churchill's plea for action against a dictator, but the point Churchill made remains vitally important – the greatest incentive to action is often and unfortunately self-preservation. So Atticus acted with a resolution that Churchill would have

Career Turbulence

most likely approved but on a course that Churchill clearly would have condemned.

Cicero, with Atticus — not Churchill — as his advisor, unfortunately dawdled until he could wait no longer to act. Cicero belatedly determined that his loyalty lay with the Optimates, left Rome, and joined Pompey at his military camp to help wage war against Caesar and to defend the Republic. Cicero would certainly have gained Churchill's approval for the course he chose but condemnation for his lack of timely resolution.

Nepos on Atticus and Caesar

> (7.3) "Atticus' neutrality so gratified Caesar, that after his victory, when he made a written demand of contributions from private citizens, he ... caused Atticus no trouble, but he even granted to his entreaties the pardon of his nephew and of Quintus Cicero, who were in Pompey's camp. Thus by the long-standing policy of his life he (Atticus) avoided new dangers."

We see that at this point in his biography, Nepos has anointed the pragmatism of Atticus, which he described as "the long standing policy of his (Atticus') life," a virtue that allowed Atticus to avoid "new dangers." As simple as this sounds we must realize that the neutrality of Atticus in this instance was a very risky gambit. As mentioned earlier, if Pompey won, Atticus could have attempted to claim that he was too old to have followed in Pompey's wake when he departed Rome (and Italy), but there were no guarantees that the excuse would have been believed, let alone accepted.

Alternatively, for Caesar and his faction, Atticus' neutrality was tantamount to deciding for Caesar, since Caesar was the one rebelling against the Senate and the Republic. Therefore it is easy to see why Caesar was so pleased with the neutrality of Atticus; since Atticus was perhaps the most powerful equestrian in Rome, and since he did not overtly demonstrate support for Pompey, he was setting an example that other businessmen could follow. Perhaps they, too, would see that Caesar was not so radical as to disturb the ongoing business interests of the equestrians.

Atticus Earns Caesar's Gratitude

Atticus' neutrality was a valuable asset for Caesar, and so Atticus reaped the rewards of his winning bet – his life as well as his fortune remained intact because of Caesar's gratitude. Additionally Caesar was so pleased with Atticus' action, or rather inaction, that he agreed to free a nephew of Atticus' and Cicero's younger brother Quintus, who was married to Atticus' sister.

Whether or not Atticus truly believed Caesar was ultimately the best choice for the state, we know that his native pragmatism meant that he would simply adjust to the new regime and that he was more than willing to accept the perquisites that came with his acceptance of Caesar's governance. In fact Atticus must have given just that advice to Cicero, for Cicero glumly wrote to Atticus in 47 BC, "You tell me to suit my looks and language to present conditions."[105] Apparently a far more difficult chore for Cicero than for Atticus!

Career Turbulence

Lesson 15: Adapt as Circumstances Demand

Atticus clearly knew the importance of adapting when it came to survival. This capability was recognized by Charles Darwin as critical to the survival of a species and is famously summarized as follows: "It is not the strongest of the species that survives, nor the most intelligent that survives. It is the one that is the most adaptable to change."[106]

Figure 4.5: Charles Darwin, author of the famous 1859 text, On the Origin of the Species.[107]

Lesson Summary

In the face of evolving markets or shifting political forces the businessperson who adopts rigidity and rejects adaptation is not being resolute but foolish and shortsighted. The ability, when necessary, to successfully navigate a course between adaptation (Atticus) and absolutism (Cicero) is a skill that must be mastered early or you risk failure and being perceived alternatively either as too vacillating

Atticus and the Caesarian Regime

Following Caesar's victory, Atticus, with his uncanny ability to adapt, his experience in war-torn Athens, and his contact with Caesar's advisors, likely provided assistance to the new regime as it wrestled with its post-civil war finances. It has even been suggested that Atticus may have been responsible for the formulation of Caesar's moderate economic policies.[108] This assistance to Caesar would have been very beneficial for Atticus, who in return for his help would have developed even stronger connections with the new regime.

Atticus and Cleopatra

Perhaps the best indicator just how far those inroads of Atticus extended, can be seen in a letter from Cicero to Atticus discussing an incident that occurred when Cleopatra, Queen of Egypt and Caesar's mistress, was staying in Rome.[109] Cicero was fulminating to Atticus about a broken promise by Cleopatra in a literary matter as well as the insolence of one of her staff during a visit to Cicero's house. Cicero was particularly furious that when he enquired of his visitor, "... in a friendly way what I could do for him he replied that he was looking for Atticus!"[110] Clearly Atticus had successfully wormed his way into the deepest recesses of Caesar's retinue.

Career Turbulence

Figure 4.6: Shows a marble bust of Cleopatra circa 40BC-30BC (Altes Museum, Berlin).[111]

Cicero's Plight

Cicero, in the wake of Caesar's victory over Pompey, was desperately in need of funds and requested of his banker Atticus, "... please, as far as you can, consider how to provide me with a sum I can draw upon for necessary expenses. Such funds as I had available I made over to Pompey at a time when this seemed a prudent thing to do."[112] Cicero, unlike his friend Atticus, risked his life and his treasure (Cicero had 2,200,000 sesterces of which Cicero gave half to Pompey) in support of the cause of the Republic and in the end found himself beholden to Caesar for clemency and Atticus for funding. Cicero had bravely put his money where his mouth was and lost.

4 - Wealth Preservation in Rome

Caesar and Cicero

Caesar, however, wanted Cicero's public support, no matter how grudging, and what Caesar wanted - he got. In a letter from Cicero to Atticus in December of 45 BC, Cicero describes his hosting a dinner for the dictator and dealing with the two thousand soldiers that traveled with him. Cicero wrote: "Strange that so onerous a guest should leave a memory not disagreeable! It was really very pleasant. ... In a word, I showed I knew how to live. But my guest was not the kind of person to whom one says, 'Do come again when you are next in the neighborhood.' Once is enough. We talked of nothing serious, but a good deal on literary matters. All in all he was pleased and enjoyed himself. ... There you are – a visit, or should I call it a billeting, which as I said was troublesome to me but not disagreeable."[113]

Chapter Review

Between 60 BC and 45 BC the Republic ultimately succumbed to the rule of major power brokers (see Figure 4.7 below for a stakeholder matrix for this period in Atticus' life), suffered civil war and finally Caesar's dictatorship.

Stakeholder Influence	60BC – 49BC	48 BC – 45BC
Significant (e.g. Keep Satisfied)	Pompey Crassus Caesar	Caesar
Moderate (e.g. Keep Informed)	Cicero Antony Brutus	Cicero Antony Brutus
Little or None (e.g. Keep in Contact)		Octavian

Figure 4.7: Shows a matrix of Atticus' potential relationships with the key powerbrokers during the years 60BC to 45BC.

Career Turbulence

The critical career preservation lessons that emerged from examining Atticus' innate ability to "keep to the inner row" during these tumultuous years, are as follows:

Lesson 12: Skepticism is a Virtue

For historians and scientists, skepticism is considered a virtue, and should be no less valued in the pursuit of job preservation.

Lesson 13: Keep your Passions in Check

Be passionate about what you do, but pragmatic in how you do it. Hard work without passion quickly leads to boredom, just as surely as passion without hard work, leads to dissolution and failure.

Lesson 14: The Deferral of Difficult Decisions Courts Disaster

Do not procrastinate in making the hard decisions. Difficult decisions are too frequently deferred until they can be delayed no longer (remember the wisdom of good time management above), often with the result that an earlier and albeit painful resolution of a problem must then be replaced with a solution that is even more gut wrenching and less certain of success. Procrastination of critical decisions for no other reasons than that they are difficult is simply a guarantee that the choice of alternatives will be reduced, and the opportunity for a successful resolution of the issues at hand diminished.

Lesson 15: Adapt as Circumstances Demand

Learn to adapt! Adaptation in the business world is an intellectual process and is therefore best accomplished with the mind if not with the heart. Change, whether personal or organizational is just plain hard, and often very emotional. Be prepared to undertake the work involved and see any change through to its completion. Alternatively, if you recognize that you have embarked on the wrong course, admit the error as soon as possible, and move to the correct path as early as it is recognized and feasible. Steadfast in failure is not a testament to resolute determination, but rather it is just a demonstration of stupidity.

Career Turbulence

CHAPTER 5

The Ides of March and Its Aftermath

Timeline for Major Events in this Chapter (44 BC)

Date (BC)	Major Event	Age of Atticus
44	Caesar's Assassination Conspiracy Led by Brutus and Cassius Octavius Adopted by Caesar in his Will Mark Antony Becomes Consul Death of Atticus' Wife Pilia Early Stages of Civil War	65

Period Background

In late January or early February of 44 BC Caesar's initial ten-year appointment as Dictator of the Roman Republic was extended. By order of the Senate, Caesar was anointed dictator for life. However, that lifelong term came to an abrupt end

Career Turbulence

within just weeks of its award. On the Ides of March (March 15th) a conspiracy, consisting of perhaps as many as sixty Senators, carried out the murder of the dictator.[114] The ancient Roman historian Dio Cassius, writing in the second and third centuries AD noted, "There is no need to give a full list of the names, for I might thus become wearisome."[115] Even if the number of conspirators was exaggerated by ancient authors in order to make the point that the resentment against Caesar ran deep, the fact that there was a large conspiracy meant it could not remain cloaked in secrecy indefinitely.

Caesar's Assassination - The Prelude

Marcus Brutus and Gaius Cassius led the assassination conspiracy and according to Plutarch's biography of Caesar, news of the plot to murder Caesar at a meeting of the Senate began to leak. For the Senate meeting on the Ides of March in 44 BC, the Senate had arranged for Pompey's theater complex - whose display of art was selected by Atticus – to serve as the "senate-house" because the official senate-house had yet to be rebuilt after it had been burned down. Plutarch wrote that:

> "A certain seer warned Caesar to be on his guard against a great peril on the day of the month which the Romans call the Ides; and when the day had come and Caesar was on his way to the senate-house, Caesar greeted the seer with a jest and said: "Well, the Ides of March have come," and the seer said softly, "Aye, they are come, but they are not gone." [116]

5 - The Ides of March and its Aftermath

The story may have the benefit of the theatrical hindsight of Plutarch who wrote of Caesar's life and death nearly 150 years after the bloody event, but the seer's warning whether real or fictitious is indicative of a breakdown in secrecy that forced the conspirators to act. So upon Caesar's arrival in the senate-house on the Ides, when he was seated in his golden chair, the conspirators crowded around the dictator, drew their daggers, and struck.

Figure 5.1: Senators surround the dictator Caesar in Pompey's Theater on the ides of March (1865 painting by Karl Theodor von Piloty). [117]

Caesar's Assassination- The Attack

Caesar stabbed back at an attacker with his stylus but then Caesar:

> "sank, either by chance or because he was pushed there by his murderers, against the pedestal on which the statue of Pompey stood. And the pedestal was drenched in his blood, so that one might have thought that Pompey

Career Turbulence

himself was presiding over this vengeance upon his enemy ... For it is said that he received twenty-three (wounds)." [118]

Figure 5.2: Shows Caesar's assassination at the foot of Pompey's statue (painting by Vincenzo Camuccini done in 1804 or 1805).[119] *Caesar, according to Plutarch was stabbed 23 times. Atticus had assisted Pompey the Great in the choice of the artwork displayed in the theater.*

Caesar's Assassination- The Aftermath

When the deed was done, and before the Senators hurriedly exited the scene of the murder:

> "Marcus Brutus immediately lifted up on high his bloody dagger, and called Cicero by name; and congratulated him on liberty being recovered."[120]

The attendence of Cicero at the assassination is still debated by some scholars so, despite Brutus' words, it is unclear from this passage whether Cicero was actually attending this session of the Senate and thus an eyewitness of the slaughter (Cicero's letters are silent on the point).

5 - The Ides of March and its Aftermath

Figure 5.3: Shows Caesar's assassins excitedly exiting the Theatre of Pompey (1867 painting by Jean-Léon Gérôme). [121] *Caesar's body, covered by his toga that he draped over himself as he was stabbed, lies at the base of the Statue of Pompey.*

Cicero Accused by Antony of Foreknowledge of the Murder

Later, when accused of foreknowledge of the event by Caesar's deputy (and Consul) Mark Antony, Cicero responded, "For who ever heard my name mentioned as an accomplice in that most glorious action?"[122] Clearly Cicero was not disappointed in the murder of Caesar but he always maintained ignorance of any foreknowledge of the deed.

Interestingly the hands of Mark Antony were not unstained; according to Plutarch, Cicero's accuser had been cautiously approached very early in the assassination planning by one of the conspirators, and it was reported, "… that Antony very well understood him (the conspirator), but did not encourage it; however, he said nothing of it, but had kept the secret faithfully."[123] Other so-called friends of Caesar as well as forgiven enemies actively participated in the murder with drawn daggers, but Antony's silence cut deep. So much for the most trusted of Caesar's deputies.

Caesar's Will

Caesar had an unmatched legacy of victory in life that continued even after his death. For Caesar from the grave struck back when his will was read and there were two cataclysmic surprises for his assassins, the people of Rome, and his family. First, Caesar left every male citizen of Rome 300 sesterces engendering mass public sympathy for the fallen dictator.[124] Caesar's action was both breathtaking and a powerful declaration – for Caesar, through his will, looked to establish himself as patron of every male citizen of Rome. Thus Caesar, in death, further enraged the masses in Rome against his killers, and in their anger they tore one suspected assassin limb from limb and they also attempted to burn down the houses of Brutus and Cassius, forcing the leaders of the conspiracy to quickly exit Rome.

The second surprise, with a much more lasting impact, was that Caesar at the end of his will indicated that upon his death "he adopted (his grand nephew) Gaius Octavius into his family and gave him his name."[125] Gaius Octavius, a mere boy of eighteen was, by his adoption, now to be called Gaius Julius Caesar Octavianus – hereafter referred to as Octavian. Over the course of the next two decades as Caesar's adopted son, and heir to Caesar's powerful legacy, Octavian would wage two civil wars. One war to avenge his adopted father's murder, and the second, for supreme power in Rome,

5 - The Ides of March and its Aftermath

with the result that the young man would see all of Caesar's assassins perish, along with Cicero's beloved Republic; for Caesar's adopted son grew up to be known as Gaius Julius Caesar Octavianus Augustus, the first and longest ruling emperor of imperial Rome.

Nepos on the Government in Play

(8.1) "There followed that period after the death of Caesar, when the government was apparently in the hands of the Brutuses (Marcus and Decimus Brutus)[126] and Cassius."

In section 8.1 above Nepos barely mentions the death of Caesar and does not call it an assassination. Nepos' silence here is deafening and clearly indicative of where his personal sympathies lay – with the Optimates and not the Caesarians. Conversely, the voluble Cicero, as we saw above, describes the event as "glorious" (a term he again used in a letter sent to Atticus on April 10, 44 BC, less than a month after Caesar's murder). Cicero writes to Atticus in one of the few letters we have of this critical period, "Our heroes achieved all that lay with themselves most gloriously and magnificently."[127] Since Nepos sheds no light on Atticus' reaction to the assassination we must use Cicero as our source for an insight into Atticus' state of mind at the time of the event. Note that in the April 10th letter Cicero stated "our" heroes using the plural possessive pronoun. Brutus, Cassius and the rest were not just Cicero's heroes; they were, at least according to Cicero, Atticus' heroes as well.

Career Turbulence

Atticus and the Conspiracy

The sheer number of these "heroes" (Plutarch's sixty) inexorably leads to the question of what Atticus knew of the conspiracy. Atticus' clients included powerful senators of the Optimates faction and his very close friend and confidant, as we will see below, was Marcus Brutus himself – the co-leader of the conspiracy to assassinate Caesar. It is therefore very difficult to imagine that a man of Atticus' intelligence with so wide a network of senatorial friends would have been completely in the dark about the planning of a conspiracy of such scale, even if the number of assassins has been grossly overstated.

Cicero, as we saw above, claimed innocence of any advance knowledge of the planning (and given Cicero's tendency to run off at the mouth it is no surprise the conspirators kept him at arm's length), and so perhaps his claim is valid – clearly there is no evidence to the contrary. There is also no evidence that Atticus was aware of the conspiracy, but given Atticus' well-documented intimacy with Brutus, his close association with many of the Optimates for whom he provided his services, and his propensity to play all sides, it is extremely difficult to fully exculpate Atticus from foreknowledge of the assassination.

Lesson 16: Keep your Ears Open

The lesson obtained from Atticus in this instance, applicable for employees at all levels of an organization, is much more mundane than the taking down of a leader: in all situations, especially those that are most challenging and risky, remember

5 - The Ides of March and its Aftermath

to emulate Atticus and function as a politician would by keeping your ears open (and your mouth shut). H. L. Mencken, one of the most influential cultural critics of the early 20th century reminded his readers exactly that when he bitingly defined a politician as "an animal which can sit on a fence and yet keep both ears to the ground."[128]

Figure 5.4: H. L. Mencken was a well-known and controversial twentieth century American columnist, critic and author.[129]

Lesson Summary

With Mencken's definition in hand, we can surely see that Atticus, Cicero's acknowledged fence-sitting friend, met Mencken's definition of a politician. Advance knowledge of any emerging crisis is a priceless asset that provides a greater opportunity to react and to even influence events in such a way that the probability of job preservation can possibly be increased.

Career Turbulence

Murder and Miscalculation

Brutus and the other conspirators had no plan for the aftermath Caesar's murder other than naively assuming that the Republic they so loved would simply re-emerge intact under the Senate's leadership once the dictator was dead. However, Caesar's 'death grip' on the government did not devolve as easily as anticipated. Caesar's deputy, and co-consul at that time, was Mark Antony who initially sought a compromise between the aristocrats that had supported the execution of Caesar and the Caesarians who sought revenge. After his initial fear for his own safety subsided (Brutus had vetoed Antony's assassination along with Caesar's ethically reasoning that they were killing a tyrant, not committing murder), Antony convened a meeting of the Senate. At that session Antony quickly (before Caesar's public funeral was held) gained approval for a middle course. An act of oblivion (the ancient equivalent of a pardon) for the conspirators was passed, as was a resolution approving all of Caesar's acts as dictator. Also the Senate voted that "Caesar would be worshiped as a divinity."[130]

These acts freed Brutus (as well as all the other conspirators) from any legal responsibility for the murder, facilitated Brutus' return to Rome, and also conveniently allowed Antony to continue in office now as the sole consul of the Republic (with all of the deified Caesar's acts remaining in force). Cicero feared for the Republic under Antony's leadership and was opposed to the resolution approving all of Caesar's acts, especially the codifying of Antony's control of the government. Cicero, in a letter to Atticus written on April 17, 44 BC vehemently

5 - The Ides of March and its Aftermath

complained that, "The tyranny lives on, the tyrant is dead! We rejoice at his slaughter – and defend his acts!"[131]

Nepos on Atticus and Brutus

(8.2) "Atticus' relations with Marcus Brutus were such, that there were none of his own age with whom the younger man was more intimate than with the old knight, whom he made, not only his chief advisor, but also his boon companion."

Here in section 8.2 we see that Nepos is intent on highlighting the relationship Atticus had with the lead assassin and appears to present an Atticus whose actions are not those of a man of muddled opinions about the deeds committed on Ides of March. If Atticus' post-Ides relationship with Brutus was public, we must conclude that Atticus was sufficiently confident in the correctness of the action of the assassins and in its aftermath, to have moved from his typical behind the scenes manipulations to uncharacteristically assuming a public position of confidant and advisor to Brutus. But even the ever-cautious Atticus could have miscalculated, and perhaps his early reaction to the assassination of Julius Caesar showed his hand too soon. For Nepos next tells us power soon swung away from Brutus and the conspirators and apparently so did Atticus.

Atticus Looks to Safeguard his Position

Atticus was usually so sure-footed in his alignment with the powerful that we must assume that in the period immediately following Caesar's death, Atticus may have yielded to his passions (as noted earlier

Career Turbulence

as an unreliable compass) and then was initially surprised by the events unleashed by Caesar's will. However, as we shall soon see, any potential misjudgments by Atticus did not last long.

Lesson 17: Do not Persist in Error

Atticus soon recognized the potential peril of too close of a proximity to the assassins following Caesar's death and quickly worked to mitigate his risks. This lesson from Atticus on error management was actually reinforced in a speech made by Cicero to the Roman Senate condemning Mark Antony following the assassination of Caesar. Cicero said, "Any man is liable to make a mistake, but no one but a downright fool will persist in error."[132] However, unlike Atticus, Cicero himself failed to follow his own advice.

Lesson Summary

The simple fact is that none of us infallible. Mistakes are made at various times in everyone's career so the key is to learn how to survive miscalculations, errors, and failures. Cicero's advice is a good starting point – as soon as you recognize the error, stop persisting in its execution. Cicero's admonition is really just an older version of the Will Roger's adage about when you are in a hole - the first thing you must do is stop digging. Next, though, you must find your way to exit the hole you are in – this is the critical part of surviving failure.

There are no guarantees, but a skillful extrication from a miscalculation or misstep (as demonstrated by Atticus in this case) can be nearly

5 - The Ides of March and its Aftermath

as great an asset to job preservation as the art of sidestepping failures entirely. That said, if the number or size of the failures significantly outweigh the successes, as will also shortly be seen in Cicero's case, no amount of effort will tip the balance in your favor.

Figure 5.5: Shows an 18th century fresco of Cicero addressing the Roman Senate as imagined by Cesare Maccari. The crisis depicted by Maccari involved a threat to the Republic nearly two decades before Caesar's murder.[133]

Caesar's Funeral

As previously mentioned, Antony initially pursued a centrist course, but by the time of Caesar's funeral, Antony had fully realized that he had an opportunity to seize complete power if Brutus (and Cassius) could be made objects of the people's search for vengeance. This goal was accomplished by Antony, when at the end of his emotional eulogy for Caesar:

> "(Antony) took the underclothes of the dead (Caesar), and held them up, showing the stains of blood and the holes of many stabs,

Career Turbulence

calling those that had done this act villains and bloody murderers."[134]

Atticus had been very alert to the risks of a public funeral for Caesar, as shown by one of Cicero's letter's following the Ides, where Cicero, commiserating on the worsening situation in Rome, wrote to him, "Recall your own words. Don't you remember crying out that all was lost if Caesar received public burial?"[135]

Nepos on Mark Antony's Ascension

(8.5) "Not long after that, Antonius began to gain the upper hand, to such a degree that Brutus and Cassius ... in utter despair went into exile."

(8.6) "(A)fter Brutus had fallen from power and was leaving Italy (Atticus, who declined to provide a public donation to the assassins) sent him a gift of a hundred thousand sesterces; ... (and later) sent orders from Rome that three hundred thousand more be given to the regicide (Nepos here chose a term that indicated Brutus executed a king)."

Antony's oration at the funeral succeeded, the mourners became a mob, and Brutus, Cassius and their supporters were once again forced from Rome. Antony's star was rising following the public funeral of Caesar and Brutus' was rapidly fading, but Atticus, even as he prepared to turn away from Brutus, whether from loyalty or for more sinister reasons, now, after refusing to make any public contributions to the assassins, made a substantial private contribution to Brutus of 400,000 sesterces.[136] Why provide a contribution now? From a business perspective four reasons come to mind:

1. Atticus consistently avoided public action but wished to remain loyal to a close friend,

2. After declining a public donation Atticus wished to mollify Cicero and the Optimates, and this act, though private, demonstrated his dedication to the cause,

3. Atticus, hedging his bets, wished to ensure that Brutus was beholden to him if Brutus was someday returned to power, and,

4. Atticus may have intended the gift as part of what today in sports is called a head fake. In the flow of the moment when an opponent is watching your movements you intentionally move your head in a direction that is different from where you intend to take your body. Atticus would therefore have given money to Brutus just as he was preparing to move in another direction – in this case, as we shall see shortly, Antony's!

Any of these four reasons or combination thereof may have applied to Atticus' motivation for the large donation – we just do not know.

The Arrival of Caesar's Adopted Son

Following Caesar's death, the last player to arrive on the scene was Caesar's chosen heir Octavian, who arrived in Rome to claim his legacy and seek the support of all those loyal to Caesar, especially Caesar's legions and his bankers (for revenge and war required both soldiers and money). Interestingly, one early supporter of the youth was Cicero, who saw Octavian as the only workable alternative to Antony's rule. However, Cicero also believed that once Antony was dealt with, Octavian could easily be thrown aside and the Republic finally restored.

Cicero Attacks Antony

In order to humiliate and vilify Antony, Cicero brought to bear all of his oratorical weapons against Mark Antony in a series of 14 blistering speeches called the Philippics while simultaneously working to raise up Octavian. Cicero was successful and with his allies in the Senate voted Antony an enemy of the state, forcing Antony to flee Rome. It now appeared to all that Cicero, without a single legion at his command, was the savior of the Republic. However, tossing aside of Octavian would be far more problematic than the cagey Cicero had anticipated.

Nepos on Mark Antony's Fall

(9.2) "When Antony was judged a public enemy, and had left Italy, no one expected to see his power restored. Not only his personal enemies, who were then very numerous and powerful, but also those who joined his opponents and hoped to gain some advantage by injuring him persecuted his friends, tried to rob his wife Fulvia of all her possessions, and were even preparing to destroy his children."

(9.3) "Although Atticus was very intimate with Cicero and a close friend of Brutus, so far was he from being induced to help them injure Antony, that on the contrary he protected the latter's friends as much as he could in their flight from the city (to Antony's camp), and gave them what help they required."

5 - The Ides of March and its Aftermath

(9.4) "Further, to Fulvia herself, when she was distracted by lawsuits and tormented by great anxiety, he (Atticus) was so unremitting in his attentions, that she never appeared in court without Atticus."

(9.5) "(When Fulvia) was unable to negotiate a loan, (Atticus) ... lent her the money without interest and without any contract."

Atticus now must have fully recognized that events were changing so rapidly that he could not be certain of any outcome, and so he followed the safer course (the inner row) by again hedging his bets and supporting multiple players in the drama that was unfolding. Atticus' support of Brutus, regardless of the underlying motivations discussed above was not unexpected, but what Atticus did next for Antony's wife Fulvia is surprising. Atticus may have sensed that the stability of the Republic was so fragile that no position could be clearly identified as weak or strong, or perhaps had been obligated by some sort of relationship to Fulvia's family,[137] but regardless of the underlying reason or reasons, the result was that Atticus now threw some support in Antony's direction. Atticus accomplished this by publically and financially supporting Antony's wife Fulvia in court. The opportunity for that support emerged as a result of Cicero's efforts in the Senate, via his Philippics, to demand an investigation of Antony in order to undermine Antony's position and authority.[138] Atticus supported Antony's wife Fulvia, while Cicero attacked Antony!

Career Turbulence

Atticus' Strategy

A direct result of Cicero's vicious attacks on Antony was the absolute hatred of Cicero by Antony and his wife. Additionally Atticus' moves could not have been well-received by Cicero, for Atticus' strategy was now diametrically opposed to Cicero's course of action, and very well may have impeded it. The results of the opposing moves by these two friends were ultimately to be deadly for the Republic, and Cicero personally, but not Atticus, whose star would shine even brighter than before.

Atticus Takes Neutrality to a new Level

Obviously Atticus recognized that not even his intimacy with Cicero and Brutus should stand in the way of his protecting his personal interests. In past crises Atticus attempted to take no sides, but in this crisis he instead appears to have taken all sides. Atticus' approach, unlike Cicero's, is indicative of a recognition that the outcome was sufficiently in doubt that no faction could be predicted as victor.

Cicero, on the other hand, sought to make the faction of his choice victorious. Shortly after Caesar's death, on April 26, 44 BC, Cicero had written Atticus that he believed, "Neutrality, which was possible in Caesar's war, will not be possible now."[139] So in this instance the paths chosen by Atticus and Cicero diverged as each attempted to navigate the crisis at hand.

5 - The Ides of March and its Aftermath

Lesson 18: In a Crisis it is Best to Hedge your Bets

Surviving the politics of a crisis is a most uncertain undertaking and as Benjamin Disraeli (twice Prime Minister under Queen Victoria, and author) put it, "There is no gambling like politics."[140] Atticus gambled on a conservative path and tried to improve his odds of survival by hedging his bets among multiple politicians rather than following his friend's course and placing all on a single winner.

Figure 5.6: Shows a late 19th century photo of the British Prime Minister and author Benjamin Disraeli.[141] Disraeli wrote in his book Endymion of the gambling that is politics.

Lesson Summary

For the modern employee, in the often complex drama of office politics, the chances of neutrality (Lesson 8) are sometimes restricted and the ability to get out of Dodge (Lesson 3) unfeasible. Therefore, in uncertain times, the hedging of your bets on multiple powerful players (lesson 18) can be an ideal

Career Turbulence

option. With this option, however, one does run the risk of being labeled "two-faced," but that is far less damaging than failing to choose the winner and suffering the loss of your employment.

A Recap of Events

Before leaving this chapter let's quickly recap where events and the major players stood in the aftermath of the Ides of March.

Brutus

Brutus (and Cassius), leaders of the conspiracy to murder Julius Caesar, had left Rome but eventually raised an army of approximately 19 Legions (70,000 men) with the support of the Senate and Cicero.[142] Brutus claimed to seek the restoration of the Republic. (Note that Atticus had provided substantial private financial support to Brutus.)

Figure 5.7: Shows a marble bust of Marcus Brutus.[143]

5 - The Ides of March and its Aftermath

Antony

Antony at Cicero's insistence had been declared an enemy of Rome and forced to leave the city. As a deputy of Caesar, Antony initially retained the loyalty of at least four of the legions formerly commanded by Caesar.¹⁴⁴ Antony claimed to seek the restoration of the Republic. (Note that Atticus had provided financial and moral support to Antony's wife.)

Figure 5.8: Shows a marble bust of Mark Antony.¹⁴⁵

Octavian

Octavian had returned to Rome to claim his inheritance - Caesar's name and the dignity that would come from his adoption by the deified Caesar, the wealth of Caesar's vast estate, and the loyalty of Caesar's legions (under pressure from Cicero the Senate had grudgingly provided at least two legions for Octavian's command).¹⁴⁶ Octavian also proclaimed a determination that the murderers of

Career Turbulence

Julius Caesar be brought to justice, a point that Cicero naively believed could be managed. (It is important to note here that although he had not yet supported Octavian, Atticus was close to Caesar's financial advisors, and we know at this point that at least one such advisor had already made his way into Octavian's camp).[147]

Figure 5.9: Shows a marble bust of Octavian.[148]

Cicero

Cicero believed that Octavian would be an ideal means to drive a wedge between Antony and his legions. Cicero had successfully convinced the Senate to elevate the young man to the position of Consul with his own legions to command. However, not everyone agreed with Cicero's plan. Brutus wrote to Atticus "… the boy's ambition and lawlessness have been stimulated rather than checked by Cicero."[149] Cicero was immune to criticism of his strategy

5 - The Ides of March and its Aftermath

of first defeating Antony militarily by utilizing Octavian and his legions, those legions loyal to Brutus and Cassius as well as those that the youth could be pry away from Antony.

After Antony was destroyed, Cicero believed he could dispose of the boy, and Cicero would emerge as the Republic's champion, saving the state from the horrors of dictatorship and tyranny. This would be the second time Cicero saved the Republic, with the first occurring late in his consulship in 63 BC when Cicero suppressed an armed insurrection led by a disgruntled politician (depicted in Figure 5.5).[150] It is important to note that the intimacy of Atticus with Cicero appeared to remain intact even as the two men wrestled with their respective approaches to the deadly crisis that was unfolding and ensnaring them.

Figure 5.10: Shows a statue of Cicero (Copyright © 2012 alessandro0770/Shutterstock.com).[151]

Career Turbulence

Atticus

Atticus, as the government teetered in chaos and blood, and despite the death of his wife Pilia, snaked his tentacles into the camps of all the major players while his life-long friend Cicero, attempted to alter the march of history and breathe life into his beloved but mortally wounded Republic.

Chapter Review

We have seen in this chapter the need for Atticus to nimbly identify and support key stakeholders immediately following Caesar's assassination on the Ides of March. The stakeholder matrix shown in Figure 5.11 summarizes that maneuvering.

Stakeholder Influence	44 BC – Pre-Ides of March	44 BC – Post-Ides of March
Significant (e.g. Keep Satisfied)	Caesar	Antony Brutus Cicero
Moderate (e.g. Keep Informed)	Cicero Antony Brutus	Octavian
Little or None (e.g. Keep in Contact)	Octavian	

Figure 5.11: Shows a matrix of Atticus' rapidly changing focus upon key political stakeholders pre/post Caesar's murder on March 15, 44BC.

5 - The Ides of March and its Aftermath

The three lessons that emerged from examining these maneuverings of Atticus's in the immediate aftermath of Caesar's death and his delicate balancing act among all the varying powerbrokers during the early stages of the civil war that followed are:

Lesson 16: Keep your Ears Open

A successful politician must learn that it is often more important to listen than to speak. Far too often politicians listen best to themselves, and that approach better suits the fool rather than the survivor. Never turn a deaf ear to the network of friends and associates you have worked so hard to build.

Lesson 17: Do Not Persist in Error

Everyone makes mistakes; but learn to recognize them early and correct them as soon as feasible. If the mistake cannot be corrected, determine the best means of damage control. The most successful approach, however, is to ensure the truth emerges quickly and in its entirety – anything less is an invitation to disaster.

Lesson 18: In a Crisis it is Best to Hedge your Bets

Take the time to understand and quantify the risks associated with any undertaking, and when it comes to the politics of a situation, remember you are always playing a game of chance and nothing is certain.

Career Turbulence

CHAPTER 6

The End Game for Cicero and Atticus

Timeline for Major Events in this Chapter (43 BC – 33 BC)

Date (BC)	Major Event	Age of Atticus
43	Cicero' Executed	66
42	Defeat and Suicide of Brutus and Cassius Empire Led by Octavian, Antony and Lepidus (Called the Second Triumvirate)	67
37	Atticus' Daughter Marries Agrippa	72

Career Turbulence

Period Background

Cicero's plan for the Republic was certainly complex and fraught with risk, but still a plan that just might work, except for two not so minor details – Octavian's determination to avenge the murder of his adoptive father, and his desire to be treated with the dignity that the adopted son of Julius Caesar deserved. The ancient Roman historian, Suetonius, wrote that the youth resented:

> "that some had called him a boy, while others (in this particular instance the foolishly loquacious Cicero) had openly said that he ought to be honoured and got rid of."[152]

And so with the demand of justice for the murderers of Caesar, and with his stated need for the preservation of his family's dignity, the "boy" with cold calculation resolved his differences with Antony and switched his allegiance from Cicero and the Senate to Antony. Antony and Octavian successfully reunited the Caesarian forces and agreed to form a Second Triumvirate (following in the footsteps of Caesar, Pompey, and Crassus), which spelled doom -- not just to Cicero's plan and Cicero himself, but for his beloved Republic, as well.

We pick up Nepos' narrative with Mark Antony's return to Rome, now the senior partner of a Second Triumvirate consisting of himself, Octavian, and a third, partner named Lepidus (a powerful military commander of Caesar's legions). The Triumvirs wasted no time in proscribing their enemies, for there was revenge to be had and fortunes to be confiscated in order to pay for the legions required

6 - The End Game of Cicero and Atticus

to defeat the forces of Brutus and Cassius. A proscribed individual could be killed on sight by anyone (with a reward given to the executioner) and the property of the proscribed confiscated by the state (another deadly lesson well learned from Sulla who demonstrated the "effectiveness" of large-scale proscriptions).

Nepos on Antony's Re-Ascension

(10.1) "There came a sudden change of fortune. Antony returned to Italy, and ... Atticus was in extreme danger because of his intimacy with Cicero and Brutus."

(10.4) "Antony felt such hatred of Cicero that he was the personal enemy, not only of the orator himself, but of all his friends, and desired to proscribe them – a course to which many urged him. But nevertheless he was mindful of the services rendered him by Atticus. Therefore when he learned where Atticus was, he wrote to him with his own hand, telling him not to be afraid."

Unfortunately for Cicero, once his plans unraveled, his chances of survival were nil. In fact, of the estimated 300 Senators proscribed,[153] Cicero was in the first wave of those to be killed (a group of twelve or perhaps seventeen),[154] Cicero, after his attacks on Antony, could not have been surprised at his death sentence at the hands of the Triumvirs (supposedly Octavian had argued strenuously to spare Cicero's life but eventually yielded to Antony).

Career Turbulence

Cicero's Execution

Plutarch describes Cicero's bloody death on December 7, 43 BC in horrifying detail. Cicero was trying to escape his villa in an enclosed litter when a centurion named Herennius and his soldiers found him. Cicero courageously stuck his neck out of the litter in which he was being carried and then Cicero:

> "clasping his chin with his left hand, as was his wont, looked steadfastly at his slayers stretched his neck forth from the litter and ... Herennius cut off his head, by Antony's command, and his hands – the hands with which he wrote the Philippics (against Antony)."[155]

The head and hands were transported to Antony in Rome but unfortunately death was not the end of the punishment for Cicero. Antony's wife Fulvia, the woman whom Atticus had stepped forward to support as well as protect and,

> "took the head into her hands before it was removed (for public display in the forum where Cicero had gained his fame), and after abusing it spitefully and spitting upon it, set it on her knees, opened the mouth, and pulled out the tongue, which she pierced with the pins that she used for her hair." [156]

6 - The End Game of Cicero and Atticus

The Fate of Atticus

Atticus was deservedly fearful, for not only was he fabulously wealthy, but, more ominously, as Nepos states in 10.1 above, his closest friends were Cicero and Brutus – under the current circumstances a very unlucky combination, indeed. Atticus stayed away from the forum in Rome and awaited his fate, but Antony was at least "mindful" of Atticus' support of his wife, Fulvia, when Antony's fortunes were at low ebb, and so Atticus was grudgingly spared (although 2,000 other equestrians were not as fortunate as the Atticus).[157] Thus Atticus' strategy of hedging his bets by looking beyond the current wielder of power paid a huge dividend – Atticus preserved his life and his wealth.

Lesson 19: Politics is More Marathon than Sprint

Once again Atticus demonstrated that in a time of uncertainty the best choice is sometimes a road not taken. Multiple options, if they can be maintained, are superior to the quick selection of one option when there is not enough information to make an informed decision. The playwright and author of the classic *1984*, George Orwell, (from whom the term "Orwellian" and description of government as "big brother" are now part of the common vernacular) provides an important reminder, which also serves as a corollary to Lesson 18 on the gamble of office politics. Orwell wrote of the seduction of the currently popular and/or powerful and noted that, "Whoever is winning at the moment will always seem to be invincible."[158]

Career Turbulence

Figure 6.1: Shows an early 20th century photo of the novelist Eric Arthur Blair who wrote his novels Nineteen Eighty-Four *and* Animal Farm *under the pen name of George Orwell.*[159]

Lesson Summary

As discussed earlier, the choosing of a winner is not a simple task, and the obvious choice is not always the inevitable victor. So when faced with the difficult and complex process of determining which potential leader or crisis manager to follow, playing for time can be critical (if our oft mentioned variable time is available) and should never be dismissed as mere indecision.

Final Defeat of Brutus and Cassius

The Triumvirate, with its ironfisted control of the Senate established, ultimately raised 43 legions (200,000 men) half of which it deployed against the regicides. The combined forces of Antony and Octavian defeated Brutus and Cassius in the fall of 42 BC. Both Brutus and Cassius chose suicide to capture and death at the hands of their victorious enemies.

6 - The End Game of Cicero and Atticus

The Reputation of Brutus

Brutus' thirst for liberty and his deadly actions to end Caesar's tyranny have brought him lasting fame. Brutus aided the perpetuation of his reputation with an interesting effort in public relations, when Brutus produced the most famous coin in antiquity (shown in Figure 6.2 below), and one of the most valuable coins of today[161] – a coin commemorating the Ides of March and Brutus' role in the event.

Figure 6.2: Shows Brutus' famous Ides of March coin minted by Brutus to commemorate Caesar's assassination (Image courtesy of The British Museum Images).[163] Depicted on one side (obverse) of the silver coin,[164] are Brutus' portrait and the inscriptions BRUT IMP (short for Brutus Imperator) and L PLAET CEST (short for Lucius Plaetorius Cestianus, the mint manager that produced the coin).[165] The other side (reverse) displays the date of Caesar's assassination (EID MAR, short for the Ides of March), daggers (the tools of the regicides) and the cap of liberty given to slaves upon their manumission (here symbolizing the freedom gained by the Roman people.

Career Turbulence

The End of the Republic

Although there is much debate as to when the Republic technically expired, with the murder of Cicero and the suicide of the lead assassins of Caesar, the death throes of the Roman Republic were certainly complete. The triumvirate endured for nearly a decade (but Lepidus did not long have power, for he crossed Octavian and was fortunate to retain his life) and so Antony and Octavian split the Roman world between them in an uneasy equilibrium. And Atticus, a very experienced survivor, did not sit idle even during this relatively quiescent period.

Figure 6.3: Shows the gold coin (aureus) issued to mark the concord between Mark Antony and Octavian (Courtesy of Classical Numismatic Group, Inc. htt://www.cncoins.com).[166]

Nepos on Atticus and the Triumvirs

(12.1) "Marcus Vipsanius Agrippa, the intimate friend of the young Caesar, ... (chose) an alliance by marriage with the family of Atticus."

(12.2) "And the one who arranged the marriage ... was Marcus Antonius."

6 - The End Game of Cicero and Atticus

Atticus now reached the pinnacle of security, for he managed to have Mark Antony arrange with Octavian the marriage of Atticus' daughter to the young Triumvir's second-in-command and life-long friend, Marcus Vipsanius Agrippa (the Pantheon still seen in Rome today was first built by Agrippa, as were extensive portions of Rome's aqueducts). Atticus again hedged his bets, but with a greater wager on Octavian, than on Antony.

Figure 6.4: Shows the Pantheon[167] that was originally commissioned by Atticus' son-in-law Agrippa and rebuilt by the Emperor Hadrian in 126 AD.

Lesson 20: The Ends Justifies the Means[168]

The harsh final lesson of this chapter and this text is drawn from all the machinations of Atticus and famously written about by Niccolo Machiavelli in his masterpiece, *The Prince*. Atticus, over a lifetime of crises, never lost sight and priority of his end goal – self-preservation of life and wealth. For Atticus, self-interest outweighed the public interest (depicted in Figure 6.5 below).

Career Turbulence

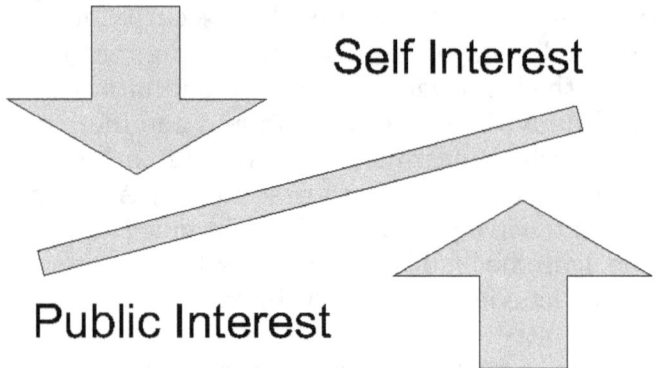

Figure 6.5: Shows the balancing required when choosing between self-interest and the public interest but for Atticus as well as Machiavelli there was no delicate balancing – both adopted the path of self-interest.

Also as clearly demonstrated by the repeated actions of Atticus, we must also always remember Machiavelli's admonition that: "Anyone who wants to act the part of a good man in all circumstances will bring about his own ruin, for those he has to deal with will not all be good."[169]

Figure 6.6: Shows a painting of Niccolo Machiavelli by Santi di Tito painted in the late 16th century.[170]

6 - The End Game of Cicero and Atticus

Lesson Summary

There is little we have seen from Nepos's account of Atticus to cause us to doubt that Atticus, especially in times of crises, would have approved of Machiavelli's acknowledgement that the ends do in fact justify the means and his recognition that saints, ensconced among sinners will indeed find self-preservation difficult if not impossible.

The implications of Lesson 20 in the business environment are harsh but pragmatic. A successful employee need not sink to the level of the sinners, but to preserve your job and career you must recognize that not everyone is virtuous and at times you must play the game, and when necessary climb down into the dirt to wrestle with your adversaries. Therefore you must always be prepared to deal with the ramifications of your actions, and the lessons of Atticus that we have studied in this handbook have been intended to assist in that preparation as well.

Chapter Review

This chapter covered the last stage of Atticus' life (and that of the Roman Republic's) during the years of 43 BC to 33 BC, a period that saw Atticus' close friend Cicero executed, the defeat and suicide of Caesar's assassins, and ultimately the joint rule of Antony and Octavian. The final stakeholder matrix emerging from the carnage of this bloody period of Roman history is shown in Figure 6.7 below.

Career Turbulence

Stakeholder Influence	43BC – 42BC	41BC – 33BC
Significant (e.g. Keep Satisfied)	Antony Brutus Cicero	Octavian
Moderate (e.g. Keep Informed)	Octavian	Antony
Little or None (e.g. Keep in Contact)		

Figure 6.7: Shows the surviving stakeholders in the final years of Atticus' life.

Our last two lessons in preserving one's wealth and career were drawn from Atticus final maneuverings and are:

Lesson 19: Politics is More Marathon than Sprint

Do not always assume in this era of instant communication and gratification that every race is a sprint – most turn out to be marathons.

Lesson 20: The Ends Justifies the Means

Self-preservation may at times require a significant degree of flexibility, for in the heat of a crisis undue moral rigidity can be transformed into brittle policy that will eventually crumble under the increasing pressure of events or the actions of those less virtuous than you.

CHAPTER 7

Atticus and his Legacy

Atticus the Author

Over the prior five chapters of this handbook we have seen how Atticus carefully navigated the course of his life, surviving the tsunamis resulting from the collapse of the Roman Republic. From Atticus' actions and reactions we were able to draw numerous lessons to help guide modern businesspeople in his/her navigation of the rough seas that suddenly can capsize even the largest of enterprises.

However, we should note that Nepos was not quite finished with Atticus, nor should we be. For Nepos in the last section of his first edition of Atticus' biography informs us that Atticus was also an author.[171] Atticus' major work, Liber Annalis (Yearly Accounts), was a book that detailed "careful lists of magistrates, of laws, of all the important events of peace and war in their chronological relation to each other and especially the history of important families through successive generations...." [172]

Career Turbulence

It is interesting to note that Atticus published his work on the chronology of major events in Rome's history under Caesar's rule. The work was thought to have been completed relatively early in Caesar's dictatorship (in 47 BC),[173] and might have served the Dictator Caesar very well, as it showed evidence of multiple periods (whether real or not) of prior Roman dictatorships.[174]

Nepos on Atticus' Literary Efforts

(18.1) "He was a great imitator of the customs of old and a lover of early time, of which he had such a thorough knowledge that he gave a full account of them in the work in which he set down the chronological order of the magistrates."

(18.2) "and – a most difficult task – he has so worked out the genealogies of he families, that from it we can learn the descendants of our famous men."

Atticus as an Apologist for the Caesarian Regime

If Atticus were an apologist for the Caesarean regime, he would have been of great value to Caesar because of his wealth, status among the equestrians, and his perceived integrity. Atticus would have, according to Professor Welch:

> "provided the Caesarian innovators with the historical 'precedents' with which they could counter criticism of the unconstitutional nature of Caesar's second dictatorship in 47 BC. The appearance of the work in this exact year, ... is simply too convenient".[175]

7 - Atticus and his Legacy

Atticus fortuitously managed to publish a work showing the existence of prior Roman dictatorships precisely at a point in time when Caesar would have most appreciated its publication!

The question we might ask ourselves is do we conclude our study of Atticus here, with the acceptance at face value of the accusation that Atticus truly sacrificed country on the altar of self-interest? Nepos (and Atticus) would certainly have hoped that his biography clearly showed otherwise, but the facts in defense of Atticus, as we have seen above, are far from conclusive. So if we again look to Cicero, perhaps we can gain further insight into Atticus' support of the Caesarians, and not simply disregard the literary work of Atticus as a mere effort to curry favor with the faction of Caesar.

Cicero's Comments on Atticus Literary Importance

Cicero, in fact, informed his readers that Atticus' work was essential to his own book entitled Brutus, a history of famous orators written in early 46 BC and presented as a dialogue among Cicero, Atticus, and Brutus.[176] Cicero wrote that Atticus' work, "afforded me exactly the help I required, to survey in one comprehensive view the whole course of things in the order of their times."[177] Clearly Atticus' work was a serious literary effort to record events and establish a firm chronology of the Roman past made much more difficult by the absence of written records predating the sack of Rome by the Gauls in 390 BC.

Career Turbulence

Cicero as an Apologist for the Caesarian Regime

Cicero too yielded to the power of the dictator. In Cicero's Brutus, published while Caesar was very much alive and in control of Rome, Cicero has Atticus say of Caesar, "… that of all our orators he is the purest user of the Latin tongue."[178] Cicero in the book's dialogue on Caesar's talents, had himself offer that, "…they are like nude figures, straight and beautiful; stripped of all ornament of style as if they had laid aside a garment."[179] But praise of Caesar's oratory was in fact warranted – Caesar was an extraordinarily talented speaker.

However, if we turn instead to the first speech made by Cicero to the dictator, in 46 BC, we find the following:

> "There is no genius so overflowing, no power of the tongue or pen so lofty or so exuberant that it can adequately describe, let alone embellish, your achievements, Gaius Caesar."[180]

Here Cicero clearly appears as fawning, and granted, two wrongs do not make a right, but if we condemn Atticus for his possible literary collaboration with the Caesarian regime so too must we condemn as well the staunch advocate of the Roman Republic, Cicero, for such over the top flattery.

7 - Atticus and his Legacy

Atticus' Genealogical Work on Brutus's Family

Interestingly, Nepos next informs us in detail of another work of Atticus. Nepos tells us that Atticus wrote of the "origin" of some of Rome's leading families. The memorializing of the pedigree of leading families would have ingratiated Atticus still further into the good graces of the major power brokers who were constantly looking for ways to puff up their dignity and that of their families to their fellow Romans. Nepos specifically mentions the effort of Atticus, at Marcus Brutus' request, to document the history of his family, the Junii.

Nepos on Atticus' Genealogies

(18.3) "He has treated this same subject by itself in other books; for example, at the request of Marcus Brutus he gave an account of the Junii in order, from their origin down to our time, noting the parentage of each member of the family and the offices which he had held, with their dates."

Perhaps this was mere pandering on Atticus' part, but then again perhaps not. For Alice Hill Byrne in her doctoral thesis completed in 1920 made a very significant observation about the importance and impact of Atticus' literary efforts on behalf of his close friend, Brutus.[181] Dr. Byrne commented that it is possible that Atticus' publication of his work on Brutus' family publicly validated Brutus' claim that he was directly descended from the ancient regicide Marcus Junius Brutus (whose actions that helped to overthrow the early monarchy were discussed in the Introduction of this text). Dr. Byrne in her thesis

Career Turbulence

indicated that this linkage by Atticus very well may have "influenced the career of Brutus and the course of history by bringing the connection into new prominence in the public mind."[182]

Brutus' Descent from the Regicide Marcus Junius Brutus

A bona fide link drawn by Atticus between Brutus and his supposed famous forebear would have placed Brutus in a very complex and difficult position. To honor the Junius Brutus who founded the Roman Republic by destroying the monarchy, Plutarch reported that:

> "... the ancient Romans erected a statue of brass among the images of the kings with a drawn sword in hand in remembrance of his courage and resolution in expelling the ... monarchy." [183]

In the presence of such a prominent monument Brutus would have been under immense pressure to live up to such an historic achievement. It was also claimed, during the dictatorship of Caesar, that upon that very statue of Junius Brutus was written the graffiti: "'O that we had a Brutus now!" and, "O that Brutus were alive!'"[184]

7 - Atticus and his Legacy

Figure 7.1: Shows a bronze bust of the regicide Lucius Junius Brutus and supposed forebear of Caesar's assassin, Marcus Junius Brutus.[185]

Brutus' Link to Caesar

Also according to Plutarch, during Caesar's civil war, Julius Caesar ordered that his commanders, if possible, avoid killing Brutus in battle.[186] Plutarch wrote:

> "And this he is believed to have done out of tenderness for Servilia, the mother of Brutus; for Caesar it seems, in his youth had been very intimate with her, and she passionately in love with him; and, considering that Brutus was born about the same time in which their loves were at the highest, Caesar had a belief that he (Brutus) was his own child."[187]

Imagine the immense added pressure such a rumor would have placed on the honorable Brutus as he wrestled with choosing his course. In fact the Roman biographer Suetonius tells us that the last words of Caesar were not Shakespeare's "Et tu, Brute?"[188] (You too, Brutus?), but rather, "You too, my child."[189]

Career Turbulence

Et tu Atticus?

As mentioned earlier, Cicero had called Atticus a "political animal"; is it then not possible that the old fox, Atticus was part lion? Was Atticus, who on the surface was the dutiful Caesarian collaborator, on a much deeper level, via his work on the family history of Brutus, a contributor or even the catalyst that finally ignited Brutus' ambitions to surpass his famous ancestor by killing the tyrant Caesar? Such an action might just prove that he, Brutus, was the legitimate heir of Junius Brutus and not the bastard son of Caesar.

Atticus' work also could have further created the opportunity for other determined assassins to pressure Brutus to join them and even lead them – for their argument would have been that the Junii family created the Roman Republic through the killing of a king[190] – could Brutus then, in his beloved Republic's time of great peril do any less for the Roman people? Today all we can do is speculate, but perhaps Cicero's most frequent correspondent played a far more dangerous and manipulative game than Nepos had recognized.[191]

Saving the Republic

We have seen that all the major participants claimed to seek the wellbeing of the Republic and each did so by his own means. Caesar wielded the sword; Brutus unsheathed the dagger; Antony proclaimed loyalty to his patron's memory; Octavian brandished his twin demands of retribution for the slain Caesar and dignity for himself; Cicero offered the power of his speech; and is it not possible that Atticus collaborated only as much as necessary and defended

7 - Atticus and his Legacy

his beloved Republic with the power of his pen? Then again, perhaps Atticus' efforts were merely another gamble in the complicated, fluid, and deadly world of Roman politics.

The Death of Atticus

Atticus' fell ill in March of 32 BC while Antony and Octavian still ruled the Roman world jointly. Rather than endure the ministrations of his physicians, Atticus decided to stop taking food, announced his intentions to die with dignity to his son-in-law Agrippa and passed away five days after making this resolution (at the age of 77).

Atticus expired shortly before Antony and Octavian waged another civil war. That war, which would have been the fourth of Atticus' generation, was famously played out with the defeat and subsequent suicide of Antony (and Cleopatra). Octavian, for the rest of his life (and also in his funerary inscription), maintained the claim that he restored the Roman Republic even while he assumed, held, and passed on to his stepson Tiberius, the mantle of Emperor.

One Final Hedge by Atticus

It should be pointed out that before Atticus died, he hedged his bets one final time and managed to betroth his granddaughter to that same stepson of Octavian, the future Emperor Tiberius (who is perhaps best known for his appointment of Pontius Pilate as Prefect of Judea). Atticus unsurprisingly managed to tie his descendents deeply to the first imperial family of Rome, and to the apex of what is

Career Turbulence

called by historians, the Augustan Age of the Roman Empire.

Figure 7.2: Shows the future Emperor Tiberius to whom Atticus betrothed his granddaughter. [192]

Nepos' and the Legacy of Atticus

Cornelius Nepos in his book *Great Generals of Foreign Nations* modestly opened his text with a dedication to Atticus that began as follows:

> "I doubt not, Atticus, that many readers will look upon this kind of writing as trivial and unworthy of the parts played by great men..."[193]

Nepos, as we mentioned earlier in this work may have been an early proponent, if not the creator of, biography as a new form of literature. Perhaps he was a bit nervous about his new genre's reception and self-consciously downplayed its importance right from the start. However, as we have seen from his efforts, Nepos provided a unique insight into Atticus'

7 - Atticus and his Legacy

life, his motivations, and his decisions. Without Nepos we would have had a much greater difficulty piecing together the legacy of Atticus from Cicero's letters alone.

From Nepos' biographical work we certainly learn much about Cicero's banker, but most critically for us we learn from Atticus how extremely difficult it is to preserve a career when major crises and conflicts loom, for they are rarely under our control, and their avoidance is more often than not wishful thinking. Therefore we, like Atticus, must always have a plan of action that allows us to respond as needed to the pressure of events.

Final Job Preservation Lesson Review

We have now seen that Atticus faced crises far more grave than we could have perhaps imagined at the start of this text, and that Atticus not only survived those challenges, but also thrived. Along the way we have observed and reviewed at length his methods, which have allowed us to formulate our set of twenty lessons. Let us review once more those lessons that emerge from studying Atticus' decades of survival during multiple civil wars sandwiched between periods of extreme political uncertainty:

1. Self-Promotion is no Vice
2. Cultivate the Powerful
3. Get the Hell out of Dodge
4. Cash is King
5. Firmness is not Synonymous with Abrasiveness

Career Turbulence

6. Do not Dismiss the Value of an Occasional Overstatement
7. Obsess about Timing
8. Consider Neutrality as an Option in a Political Conflict
9. It is Who you Know that Makes the Difference
10. Self-Preservation Trumps Trust
11. Do not Underestimate the Power of Tenacity
12. Skepticism is a Virtue
13. Keep your Passions in Check
14. The Deferral of Difficult Decision Courts Disaster
15. Adapt as Circumstances Demand
16. Keep your Ears Open
17. Do Not Persist in Error
18. In a Crisis it is Best to Hedge your Bets
19. Politics is More Marathon than Sprint
20. The Ends Justifies the Means

In summary, do as Atticus did and always be as prepared as is possible for both the expected and the unexpected, adapt as events demand and maintain an icy focus on your end goal or goals. By doing just that, despite the criticism of many historians, Atticus and his family survived the trauma of civil conflicts and the collapse of the Roman Republic. The lessons we have learned from the actions of Atticus are at times harsh, and you must determine

7 - *Atticus and his Legacy*

if and when to apply those lessons to your personal situation, but when it comes to job preservation in a crisis, you could do much worse than choosing Cicero's banker as your role model.

APPENDIX A

Additional Information on Nepos

According to John C. Rolfe, the translator of Nepos' works and the source for all Nepos quotes in this text, Nepos was born about 99 BC, most likely in the ancient town of Ticinum, then part of Cisalpine Gaul (today, modern Pavia in south-western Lombardy in Northern Italy), and Nepos is thought to have moved to Rome at an early age. Nepos was wealthy, eschewed politics, corresponded with Cicero, and was an "intimate of Atticus."[194] It would seem that "… Nepos, like his friend Atticus, was a publisher, as well as a writer, of books."[195] Nepos dedicated his book on Great Generals of Foreign Nations to Atticus and outlived his friend by approximately eight years, with Nepos' death occurring in about 24 BC.[196] The biography of Atticus was part of his work on *Roman Historians* of which little survived other than the work on Atticus. This work appears to have undergone a revision after Atticus' death in 32 BC.

Career Turbulence

Modern historians have looked poorly upon the quality of Nepos' work (a very tough crowd, they criticize both the biographer and his subject). Perhaps Nepos' harshest critic is Nicholas Horsfall, who in his 1982 commentary on Nepos and his work for the Cambridge History of Classical Literature stated, "Nepos is an intellectual pygmy whom we find associating uneasily with the literary giants of his generation. Atticus, whom Nepos called friend and to whom he dedicated his biographies, shared jokes with Cicero at Nepos' expense."[197] Possibly in an effort to say something a little positive about Nepos, Horsfall acknowledged, "To his (Nepos') credit, though, he did recognize the historical value of Cicero's works."[198] Ok, so perhaps it was not even a little positive after all. Conversely, Margaret M. Miles in her book *Art As Plunder,* argues that Nepos "represented a pioneering stage in Roman biography"[199] and that he was sufficiently familiar with Cicero's works to pattern his biography of Atticus on Cicero's speeches (See Appendix B for a further discussion of this topic).

Other recent evaluations of Nepos also tend to be a bit gentler than Horsfall, as well. For example, Frances Titchener, in her study *Cornelius Nepos* and the *Biographical Tradition* notes, "Cornelius Nepos was an unexciting but competent author who was closely acquainted with some of the most prominent figures of his day."[200] Granted, this is not exactly a ringing endorsement of Nepos' work, but at least it is better than Horsfall. For our use, the importance is not that Nepos be highly regarded, but rather a biographer sufficiently competent to assist us in the unraveling of Atticus' dealings, and in this Nepos does not fail us.

APPENDIX B

Nepos and Cicero

As we discussed in the introduction of this text, Nepos has been grudgingly credited with contributing to, if not creating, a new genre of literature with his contemporary biography of Atticus. However, Margaret M. Miles in her book *Art As Plunder*, points out that Nepos may in fact owe his friend, Cicero, a substantial literary debt. For in 70 BC, at the request of the Sicilians, Cicero prosecuted a former provincial governor of Sicily, Gaius Verres, for extortion. In his abuse of power, Verres, among many other heinous crimes also absconded with ancient works of art from Sicily. Perhaps Verres' infamous craving for ancient Greek art triggered an obvious opportunity for Nepos to compare the "bad" Verres with the "good" Atticus. And so Dr. Miles very convincingly argues that Nepos created the Atticus in his biography as an anti-Verres, based upon Cicero's searing public and published condemnation of the former Governor Verres.

Career Turbulence

In Republican Rome, Verres' trial received huge attention. After a blistering opening indictment by Cicero, Verres, rather than offering a defense, left Rome for Marsilia (modern day Marseilles, in France) where he resided in exile for over a quarter of a century until Mark Antony proscribed him (supposedly to obtain the very works of art that Cicero had prosecuted Verres for stealing). Cicero, in 70 BC, chose to publish all of his material against Verres (most of it unused in court) in a series called *The Verrines*, or *Against Gaius Verres*.

Dr. Miles developed the following list comparing Cicero's examples of Verres' malfeasance, with the morality of Atticus as presented by Nepos. Given that Nepos was writing decades after Cicero published his material condemning Verres, the long list of comparisons makes a strong case that Nepos used Cicero's work as a template for his own efforts. Dr. Miles' listing includes:

"Verres' father consorted with bribery agents, but Atticus' father loved literature; Verres was detested by foreign peoples he visits, whom he extorts and robs, but Atticus was beloved by the Athenians and loaned them money at favorable rates; Verres manipulated the grain supply in Sicily, but Atticus donated grain to hungry Athens. Verres demands and extorts honorary statues, and they are thrown down after he leaves, whereas Atticus refuses offered statues, but after he leaves the Athenians put them up anyway. Verres manipulated inheritances of strangers to his benefit, but Atticus was so pleasant to a crusty elderly uncle that he surprised him with an

Appendix B - Nepos and Cicero

unexpected inheritance. Verres' knowledge of Greek is deemed uncertain and mocked, but Atticus spoke Greek like an Athenian and was a grammatical critic in both Greek and Latin. Verres took lucrative posts abroad, abused them, and was always under suspicion, but Atticus was offered such posts abroad and refused them to avoid any suspicion. Verres' home in Rome was stuffed with looted art and he hoarded gold and silver plate, but Atticus maintained his old house as it was, with modest furnishings and tableware. Verres used dubious foreign freedman and slaves to do his dirty business, but Atticus had an excellent slave household, with slaves born there and trained by him, all of them literate. Verres held banquets with carousing and excess, attended by other men's wives, but at Atticus', one dined with friends while a reader read aloud from literary works. Verres went into ignominious exile and was proscribed by Antony, but Atticus survived the proscriptions and eventually died surrounded by friends."[201]

This exhaustive listing by Dr. Miles demonstrates that Nepos must have been very familiar with Cicero's work and was also clever enough to see the applicability of Cicero's genius to his own literary efforts. Perhaps Nepos was less of an "intellectual pygmy" than Horsfall thinks! Then again, perhaps not, because Nepos' work could also be thought to be a weak reflection of Cicero's originality and brilliance.

Career Turbulence

APPENDIX C

Cicero's Self-Censorship

An excellent example of Cicero's fear, and his need for self-censorship, is well demonstrated by a letter Cicero wrote to Atticus in July of 59 BC, not long after the ascension of the First Triumvirate of Caesar, Pompey, and Crassus:

> "Of the political situation I shall say little. I am terrified by now for fear the very paper may betray us. So henceforward, if I have occasion to write you at any length, I shall obscure my meaning with code terms. As things are, Rome is dying of a strange malady. Disapproval of what has been done and indignant complaint are universal. Opinion is not divided at any point, there is open grumbling, even to the stage of loud groaning, but nobody comes forward with a remedy. This is because we think resistance is bound to be suicidal ... I told you that I shall address my letters to 'Furius', but there is no need to change *your* name. I shall call myself 'Laelius' and you 'Atticus,' and I shall not write in my own hand or use my seal, that is if the letter is such that I should not want it to get into a strangers' hands."[202]

Career Turbulence

APPENDIX D

Atticus' Lifestyle

Both Nepos and Cicero recorded instances of the frugality of Atticus. In section 13.6-7 of his biography of Atticus, Nepos wrote:

"I shall not pass over the fact, although I suppose that some will regard it as trivial, that although he was one of the richest of the Roman knights, and with no little generosity invited to his house men of all ranks, we know from entries in his day-book that he consistently limited his expenses to not more than three thousand sesterces (approx. $12,000) each month. And this I state not from hearsay, but from actual knowledge; for because of our intimacy I was often familiar with the details of his domestic life."

In section 14.3 of his biography, Nepos reported that Atticus: "... had no gardens, no expensive villa in the suburbs or on the sea."

Career Turbulence

Cicero also documented Atticus' careful financial habits when he jokingly commented in a letter to Atticus about Atticus' penuriousness, "...you give us bits of cabbage for dinner on fern-pattern dishes."[203] Thus we see that both Cicero and Nepos had first hand knowledge of Atticus' great wealth, as well as his economical lifestyle despite that wealth.

APPENDIX E

End Notes

Chapter 1

[1] United States Courts. "Bankruptcy Statistics". Accessed January 23, 2012. <http://www.uscourts.gov/Statistics/BankruptcyStatistics.aspx>.

[2] RealtyTrac. "Record 2.9 Million U.S. Properties Receive Foreclosure Filings in 2010 Despite 30-Month Low in December". Accessed January 23, 2012. <http://www.realtytrac.com/content/press-releases/record-2.9-million-us-properties-receive-foreclosure-filings-in-2010-despite-30-month-low-in-december-6309>.

[3] John A. Byrne, with Lindsey Gerdes. "The Man Who Invented Management." *Bloomberg/Businessweek*. November 28, 2005. Accessed March 4, 2012. <http://www.businessweek.com/magazine/content/05_48/b3961001.htm>.

[4] Drucker (2006). Page 9.

Career Turbulence

5. Mark Antony in this text will be referred to as Marcus Antonius only when an ancient source is quoted.

6. See Everitt (2003). *The Life and Times of Rome's Greatest Politician, Cicero.*

7. *Cicero, Letters to Atticus.* 21.8 (II.1.8). All quotations of Cicero's letters are taken from Shackleton Bailey.

8. Welch (page 452).

9. Shackleton Bailey. *Cicero, Letters to Atticus.* (Vol. 1, p. 19).

10. Jones (2006) Page 172. Regarding population figures for equestrians and councilors.

11. See for example *The Founders and the Classics* by Carl J. Richard.

12. According to Shackleton Bailey in *Cicero, Letters to Atticus*, Vol. 1, page 2, Cicero's letters, "were probably not published until the middle of the first century A.D." and the source of the letters may very well have been the estate of Atticus.

13. Titchener (page 98).

14. This work is the only surviving example of ancient Roman biography of an individual still living when the biography was written.

15. The legend of the founding of the Roman Republic, in much greater detail, can be found in Livy 1.57-2.6.

16. This image is in the public domain.

17. Everitt (2003). Pages 19-20.

Appendix E - End Notes

[18] Nicholson (page 62).

[19] Rawson (page 293).

[20] Adapted from Everitt (2003). Pages 13-15.

Chapter 2

[21] This work is in the public domain in the United States because it is a work prepared by an officer or employee of the United States Government as part of that person's official duties.

[22] Miller (page 153).

[23] Typically, a practice where the right to collect the taxes from a territory was contracted out to a consortium of equestrians (the tax farmers) who would guarantee the collection of a percentage of the taxes that were owed the state with any overage collected retained by the consortium.

[24] This image is in the public domain. Source: User Bibi Saint-Pol. <http://en.wikipedia.org/wiki/File:Sulla>.

[25] Plutarch described him as "a man second to none in villainies." Plutarch. *Sylla* (Vol.1, page 613). All quotations of Plutarch's *Sylla* are taken from Clough.

[26] Sulpicius was murdered by one of his slaves. As a reward Sulla freed the slave and then had him executed for murdering his master.

[27] Sulla implemented proscriptions, a mechanism whereby those proscribed, along with anyone

shielding them, forfeited their life and their estate to the state.

[28] This image is in the public domain. Source: User Bibi Saint-Pol. <http://en.wikipedia.org/wiki/File:Marius_Glyptothek_Munich_319.jpg>.

[29] Nepos. *Atticus*. All translations of Nepos are taken from Rolfe.

[30] Rolfe (page 287, note 2).

[31] Noble, Holcomb B. and Martin, Douglas. *The New York Times*. (Published April 26, 2006). "John Kenneth Galbraith, 97, Dies; Economist Held a Mirror to Society". <http://www.nytimes.com/2006/04/30/obituaries/30galbraith.html>.

[32] *The Economist*. May 4, 2006. <http://www.economist.com/node/6877092>. Accessed March 15, 2012.

[33] This image is in the public domain in the United States because it is a work prepared by an officer or employee of the United States Government as part of that person's official duties.

[34] Warren Buffet. *The New York Times*. August 14, 2011. In an Op-Ed piece, Buffet sarcastically wrote: "blessings are showered upon us (the wealthy) by legislators in Washington who feel compelled to protect us, much as if we were spotted owls or some other endangered species. It's nice to have friends in high places." <http://www.nytimes.com/2011/08/15/opinion/stop-coddling-the-super-rich.html>. Accessed March 12, 2012.

Appendix E - End Notes

35   This image is in the public domain in the United States because it is a work prepared by an officer or employee of the United States Government as part of that person's official duties.

36   Shackleton Bailey. *Cicero, Letters to Atticus.* Vol. 1, page 17.

37   Nepos. Section 14.2-3. An estimate of the value of one sesterce today would be approximately four dollars. This estimate is based upon the following assumptions: one sesterce was valued at 1/100th of a gold coin called an aureus that weighed 7.3 grams during Nero's reign and if one Troy oz. weighing 31 grams is valued today at $1,700. Please note that a different gold valuation or commodity comparison (e.g. silver) would yield a different value relationship. Therefore in today's dollars Atticus would have inherited from his father (a man who was merely rich for his day) approximately $8 million.

38   Shackleton Bailey. *Cicero, Letters to Atticus.* Vol. 1, page 17.

39   Quote from the Wolf (Harvey Keitel) in the movie *Pulp Fiction* (1994). <http://www.pulpfiction.com/news-mr-wolfs-first-scene.html>. Accessed January 16, 2012.

40   Copyright Miramax. Used courtesy of the Everett Collection.

41   Anonymous. The entire adage is "revenue is vanity, margin is sanity and cash is king".

42   Courtesy of Photostock.

Career Turbulence

[43] Plutarch wrote of the sack of Athens that "There was no numbering the slain; the amount is ... conjectured only from the space of ground overflowed with blood." Plutarch. *Sylla*. Vol. 1, Page 619.

[44] Welch (page 453).

[45] Napoleon Bonaparte. <http://www.goodreads.com/quotes/show/255548>. Accessed January 12, 2012.

[46] This image is in the public domain because its copyright has expired.

[47] *Cicero, Letters to Atticus*. 121.2 (VI.6.2).

[48] Donald Trump. <http://www.successories.com/iquote/author/1298/donald-trump-quotes/1>. Accessed January 15, 2012.

[49] Courtesy of Lev Radin and Shutterstock.com. Source: <http://www.shutterstock.com/gallery-64736p1.html>.

[50] Theodore Roosevelt. <http://www.iperceptive.com/authors/theodore_roosevelt_quotes.html>. (Quoted in *The Works of Theodore Roosevelt*. 1926. Accessed March 15, 2012.

[51] This image is in the public domain because its copyright has expired.

Chapter 3

[52] Plutarch. *Sylla* (Vol. 1, page 633).

Appendix E - End Notes

53   This image is in the public domain. Courtesy of the University of Texas Libraries, The University of Texas at Austin. <http://en.wikipedia.org/wiki/File:Hw-pompey.jpg>.

54   This image is in the public domain. Source: <http://en.wikipedia.org/wiki/File:Marcus_Licinius_Crassus>.

55   Plutarch. *Caesar* (I.2). All quotes from Plutarch's *Caesar* are from Perrin.

56   This image is in the public domain. Source: Tataryn77. <http://en.wikipedia.org/wiki/File:CaesarTusculum.jpg>.

57   Additional excitement would have been engendered by the punishment of the defendant (Roscius of Ameria) if he had been convicted. The alleged crime was patricide, so Cicero's client, if found guilty, could have been sewn into a sack with a dog, monkey, cock and a snake, and then thrown into the sea.

58   Shackleton Bailey. *Cicero, Letters to Atticus*. (Vol. 1, page 17)

59   According to *Tempest* (2011, page 37), most modern scholarship discounts Plutarch's version of events, as told here, for Sulla had by the time of this trial retired from his position as dictator.

60   This image is in the public domain because its copyright has expired.

61   *The New American Bible*. Matthew 12.30. (Page 1027).

Career Turbulence

[62] John F. Kennedy remarks in Bonn, West Germany, at the signing of a charter establishing the German Peace Corps, June 24, 1963. Online by Gerhard Peters and John T. Woolley. *The American Presidents Project.* <http://www.presidency.ucsb.edu/ws/?pid=9294>.

[63] This work is in the public domain in the United States because it is a work prepared by an officer or employee of the United States Government as part of that person's official duties.

[64] *Cicero, Letters to Atticus.* 18.8 (I.18.8).

[65] Anonymous. The entire adage is "It's not what you know but who you know that makes the difference."

[66] Welch (pages 458-463).

[67] Cicero. *Letters to Quintus.* 4.1 (I.4.1). All quotes from Cicero's *Letters to Quintus* are from Shackleton-Bailey.

[68] *Cicero, Letters to Atticus.* 73.1 (IV.1.1).

[69] Cicero. *Letters to Quintus.* 4.1 (I.4.1).

[70] *The Godfather.* 1972. A scene between Tom Hagen (Robert Duvall) and Sonny Corleone (James Caan). <http://www.imdb.com/character/ch0000812/quotes>. Accessed January 16, 2012.

[71] Photo by Mary Evans/PARAMOUNT PICTURES/Ronald Grant/Everett Collection.

[72] *Cicero, Letters to Atticus.* 13.1 (I.13.1).

[73] *Cicero, Letters to Atticus.* 19.9 (I.19.9).

Appendix E - End Notes

[74] Pliny. *Natural History*. XXXV.XL.127. All quotations of Pliny the Elder's *Natural History* are taken from Rackham (Books 33-35).

[75] Napoleon Bonaparte. BrainyQuote.com, Xplore Inc, 2012. <http://www.brainyquote.com/quotes/quotes/n/napoleonbo378985.html>. Accessed January 17, 2012.

[76] This image is in the public domain because its copyright has expired.

Chapter 4

[77] Shakespeare. *Julius Caesar*. (Act 3, Scene 1, line 273).

[78] Knight is another term for an equestrian.

[79] Amount in dollars is approximately $40 Million.

[80] Valerius Maximus. *Memorable Doings and Sayings*. 7.8.5. All quotations of Valerius Maximus' *Memorable Doings and Sayings* are from Shackleton Bailey.

[81] *Cicero, Letters to Atticus*. 65.1 (III.20.1).

[82] Unsourced but attributed to J. Pierpont Morgan.

[83] This image is in the public domain because its copyright has expired.

[84] <http://www.jpmorgan.com/pages/jpmorgan/about>. Accessed June 15, 2012.

[85] Rawson (page 144).

[86] Cicero. *Letters to Quintus*. 7.7 (II.3.7).

[87] The translator here selected the French term *politique*, a word frequently used in the 16th

Career Turbulence

and 17th century for a moderate during the religious wars of the time.

[88] *Cicero, Letters to Atticus.* 82.4 (IV.8a.4).

[89] *Cicero, Letters to Atticus.* 83.2 (IV.6.2).

[90] Welch in her "Pomponius Atticus: A Banker in Politics?" (page 450) asserts this is the "most significant description given anywhere of Atticus."

[91] *Cicero, Letters to Atticus.* 97.3 (V.4.3).

[92] <http://www.merriam-webster.com/dictionary/realpolitik>. Accessed January 28, 2012.

[93] Unsourced, but attributed to Benjamin Franklin.

[94] This image is in the public domain. Source: User Dlz28. <http://en.wikipedia.org/wiki/File:Houdon_-_Benjamin_Franklin_(1778).jpg>.

[95] *Cicero, Letters to Atticus.* 124.2 (VII.1.2).

[96] *Cicero, Letters to Atticus.* 169.1 (IX.2a.1).

[97] *Cicero, Letters to Atticus.* 198.1 (X.7.1).

[98] Translation courtesy of Professor Jacqueline Carlon.

[99] *Cicero, Letters to Atticus.* 85.1 (IV.9.1).

[100] Plutarch. *Caesar.* (XXXIII.5) All quotations of Plutarch's *Caesar* are taken from Perrin.

[101] *Cicero, Letters to Atticus.* 194.1 (X.3a.1).

[102] Winston Churchill. Speech to the House of Commons, May 2, 1935. <http://www.

Appendix E - End Notes

quotationspage.com/quote/41363.html>. Accessed January 16, 2012.

[103] This image is in the public domain.

[104] Source: Nobleprize.org. <http://www.nobelprize.org/nobel_prizes/literature/laureates/1953/#>. Accessed June 16, 2012.

[105] *Cicero, Letters to Atticus.* 234.5 (XI.24.5).

[106] "The earliest known appearance of this basic statement is a paraphrase of Darwin in the writings of Leon C. Megginson, a management sociologist at Louisiana State University. Megginson's paraphrase (with slight variations) was later turned into a quotation." <http://en.wikiquote.org/wiki/Charles_Darwin>. Accessed January 16, 2012.

[107] This image is in the public domain.

[108] Welch (page 468, n98).

[109] The incident referenced in the letter took place prior to the assassination of Caesar but the letter was written a few months after the death of Caesar.

[110] *Cicero, Letters to Atticus.* 393.2 (XV.15.2).

[111] This image in the public domain.

[112] *Cicero, Letters to Atticus.* 224.4 (XI.14.4); Note 3.

[113] *Cicero, Letters to Atticus.* 353.1-2 (XIII.52.1-2).

Chapter 5

[114] Suetonius. *Caesar.* LXXX.4.

Career Turbulence

[115] Dio Cassius. *Roman History*. (Book XLIV.14.3). All quotations of Dio Cassius' *Roman History* are from Cary.

[116] Plutarch. *Caesar*. (LXIII.3-4).

[117] This image is in the public domain.

[118] Plutarch. *Caesar*. (LXVI.7).

[119] This image is in the public domain.

[120] Cicero. *The Second Philippic*. (XII). All Quotations of Cicero's *Second Philippic* are from Yonge.

[121] This image is in the public domain.

[122] Cicero. *The Second Philippic*. (XI).

[123] Plutarch. *Antony*. page 489. All Quotations of Plutarch's *Antony* are taken from Clough.

[124] Suetonius. *The Deified Julius*. (LXXXIII.2).

[125] Suetonius. *The Deified Julius*. (LXXXIII.2).

[126] Another assassin of Caesar.

[127] Cicero, *Letters to Atticus*. 358.2 (XIV.4.2).

[128] H. L. Mencken. <http://en.wikiquote.org/wiki/Politics>. Accessed March 16, 2012.

[129] This image is in the public domain because its copyright has expired.

[130] Plutarch. *Caesar*. (Page 243).

[131] *Cicero, Letters to Atticus*. 363.2 (XIV.9.2).

[132] Cicero. *Philippics*. (XII.II).

[133] This image is in the public domain because its copyright has expired. The image shows

Appendix E - End Notes

Cicero as Consul in 63 BC condemning the revolutionary Catiline who sits isolated from the other Senators.

[134] Plutarch. *Antony.* (pages 489-490).

[135] *Cicero, Letters to Atticus.* 368.3 (XIV.3).

[136] Nepos was sufficiently impressed with this generous act to have included it in the biography that was published years after the defeat and suicide of Brutus, at a time when Octavian and Antony, the Caesarian leaders, controlled the Roman world between themselves.

[137] The potential role of familial relations in Atticus' support of Fulvia was pointed to the author by Professor Jacqueline Carlon.

[138] Kramp Geweke (page 478).

[139] *Cicero, Letters to Atticus.* 376.2 (XIV.13.2).

[140] Disraeli. *Endymion.* (Chapter 82).

[141] This image is in the public domain because its copyright has expired.

[142] Everitt (2006) page 87.

[143] This image is in the public domain. Source: Marie-Lan Nguyen. <http://en.wikipedia.org/wiki/File:Portrait_Brutus_Massimo.jpg>.

[144] Everitt (2006) page 65.

[145] This image is in the public domain. Source: Tataryn77. <http://en.wikipedia.org/wiki/File:CaesarTusculum.jpg>.

[146] Everitt (2006) page 69.

Career Turbulence

147   Cicero, *Letters to Atticus*. 364.3 (XIV.10.3).

148   This image is in the public domain because its copyright has expired.

149   Cicero. *Letters to Brutus*. 26.1 (I.17.1). All quotations of Cicero's *Letters to Brutus* are taken from Hendrickson.

150   When Cicero was consul in 63 he saved the Republic from a disgruntled Senator and revolutionary Lucius Sergius Catiline.

151   Copyright © 2012 alessandro0770/ Shutterstock.com.

Chapter 6

152   Suetonius. *The Deified Augustus*. (XII.12). All quotations of Suetonius' *The Deified Augustus* are from Rolfe.

153   Appian. *Roman History*. (Bk. IV.II.5). All translations of Appian's *Roman History* are from White.

154   Appian. *Roman History*. (Bk. IV.II.6).

155   Plutarch. *Cicero*. (XLVIII.3-4).

156   Dio Cassius. *Roman History*. (Book XLVII.8.4).

157   Appian. *Roman History*. (Bk. IV.II.5).

158   *The Orwell Reader*. (Page 348).

159   This image is in the public domain. <http://www.netcharles.com/orwell/>. and <http://en.wikipedia.org/wiki/File:George_Orwell>.

160   Everitt (2006) *Augustus*. Page 87.

Appendix E - End Notes

[161] The coin, a silver denarius, sold for $546,250 at auction in 2011.

[162] The minting of this coin by Brutus, showing his face and the death of a fellow Roman, was so extraordinary that the Roman historian Dio Cassius even made note of it. (Book 47.25.3)

[163] Image of this silver denarius courtesy of The Trustees of the British Museum.

[164] About.com, part of The New York Times Company. <http://coins.about.com/od/famousrarecoinprofiles/p/eidmarprofile.htm>. Accessed July 3, 2012. Approximately sixty of the silver denarius specimens are thought to still exist and two in gold, although it is now believed that one of the two gold aureus versions is a fake.

[165] About.com, part of The New York Times Company. <http://coins.about.com/od/famousrarecoinprofiles/p/eidmarprofile.htm>. Accessed July 3, 2012.

[166] Courtesy of Classical Numismatic Group, Inc. <http://www.cngcoins.com>.

[167] This image is in the public domain.

[168] An old Italian proverb. <http://www.italiansrus.com/proverbs/proverb45.htm>. Accessed November, 27, 2012.

[169] Machiavelli. *The Prince*. (Chapter 15, page 48).

[170] This image is in the public domain. <http://en.wikipedia.org/wiki/File:Portrait_of_Niccolò_Machiavelli_by_Santi_di_Tito.jpg>.

Career Turbulence

Chapter 7

[171] We know there was a second edition because in the derivatives of the manuscripts that we have, Nepos opens Section 19 of his text with the following, "Here ends what I wrote during the lifetime of Atticus. Now since it was fortune's decree that I should survive him, I will finish the account..."

[172] Hendrickson (page 6).

[173] Welch (page 468).

[174] Welch (page 469).

[175] Welch (page 469).

[176] Hendrickson (page 5).

[177] Cicero. *Brutus* (15). All quotations of Cicero's *Brutus* are from Hendrickson.

[178] Cicero. *Brutus* (252).

[179] Cicero. *Brutus* (262).

[180] Cicero. *Pro Marcello* (4).

[181] Byrne (1920).

[182] Byrne (page 39).

[183] Plutarch. *Marcus Brutus* (page 572). All quotes from Plutarch's *Lives: Marcus Brutus* are from Clough.

[184] Plutarch. *Marcus Brutus*. (Page 578).

[185] This image is in the public domain. <http://en.wikipedia.org/wiki/File:Capitoline_Brutus_Musei_Capitolini_MC1183.jpg>.

[186] Plutarch. *Marcus Brutus* (page 575).

Appendix E - End Notes

[187] Plutarch. *Marcus Brutus* (page 575). Scholars doubt Plutarch here as Caesar, at the time of Brutus' birth, would have only been about 15 years old.

[188] Shakespeare. Act III Scene I.

[189] Suetonius. *The Deified Julius.* LXXXII.3.

[190] Since Junius Brutus also killed two of his own sons for conspiring with the tyrants, Caesar's adherents following his assassination claimed that Marcus Brutus was instead descended from a plebeian that only later rose to high office. Brutus' admirers argued that Junius Brutus had a third male child, a mere infant that survived and sired the lineage leading to Marcus Brutus. Plutarch. *Marcus Brutus* (page 573). Hence we see the importance of Atticus' study.

[191] Cicero too, in his work *Brutus* does not hesitate to remind his friend Marcus Brutus early in his fictional dialogue that the "founder of your noble family ... drove from the state a powerful king ... freeing it from the domination of an absolute ruler." (*Brutus*, 53).

[192] This image is in the public domain.

[193] Nepos. *Great Generals of Foreign Nations.* Preface.

Appendix A

[194] Rolfe (page viii).

[195] Rolfe (page viii).

[196] Rolfe (page vii).

Career Turbulence

[197] Horsfall (290).
[198] Horsfall (page 292).
[199] Miles (page 230).
[200] Titchener (page 98).

Appendix B
[201] Miles (pages 229-230).

Appendix C
[202] Cicero, *Letters to Atticus*. 40.3-5 (II.20.3-5).

Appendix D
[203] Cicero, *Letters to Atticus*. 115.3 (VI.1.13).

APPENDIX F

Bibliography

Ancient Sources

Appian. *Roman History*. Trans. Horace White. Vols. III-IV. Cambridge: Harvard University Press, 1913.

Caesar. *The Civil War*. Trans. Jane P. Gardner. New York: Penguin Books, 1976.

Caesar. *The Conquest of Gaul*. Trans. S.A. Handford. New York: Penguin Books, 1982.

Cicero. *Brutus*. Trans., G.L. Hendrickson. Cambridge: Harvard University Press, 1962.

Cicero. *Letters to Atticus*. Trans. D.R. Shackleton Bailey. Vols. I, II, III, IV. Cambridge: Harvard University Press, 1999.

Cicero. *Letters to Quintus and Brutus*. Trans. D.R. Shackleton Bailey. Cambridge: Harvard University Press, 2002.

Cicero. *On Duties.* Trans. Walter Miller. Cambridge: Harvard University Press, 2005.

Cicero. *Orations Pro Marcello.* Trans. N. H. Watts. Cambridge: Harvard University Press, 1953.

Cicero. *The Fourteen Orations (Philippics) Against Marcus Antonius.* Trans. C.D. Yonge. Digireads.com Publishing, 2009.

Cornelius Nepos. *Latin Historians.* Trans. John C. Rolfe. Cambridge: Harvard University Press, 2005.

Dio Cassius. *Roman History.* Trans. Earnest Cary. Vols. III-V. Cambridge: Harvard University Press, 2005.

Livy. *The Early History of Rome.* Trans. Aubrey de Selincourt. London: Penguin Books.

Pliny the Elder. *Natural History.* Trans. H. Rackham. Vol. IX. Cambridge: Harvard University Press, 1999.

Plutarch. *Lives.* Trans. Arthur Hugh Clough. Vols. I and II. New York: Random House, Inc., 2001.

Plutarch. *Lives.* Trans. Bernadotte Perrin. Cambridge: Harvard University Press, 1919.

Seneca the Elder. *Suasoriae.* Trans. William A. Edward. London: Bristol Classical Press, 2006.

Suetonius. *The Twelve Caesars.* Trans. John C. Rolfe. Vol. I. Cambridge: Harvard University Press, 2001.

Valerius Maximus. *Memorable Doings and Sayings.*
    Trans. D.R. Shackleton Bailey. Vol. II.
    Cambridge: Harvard University Press,
    2000.

Secondary Sources

Andreau, J. *Banking and Business in the Roman World.* Cambridge: Cambridge University Press, 1999.

Babcock, Charles L. "The Early Career of Fulvia." *The American Journal of Philology.* Vo. 86, No. 1 (Jan. 1965), pp. 1-32. The John Hopkins University Press. <http://www.jstor.org/stable/292619>. Accessed September 2, 2012.

Beesley, A. H. *The Gracchi Marius and Sulla.* Kessinger Publishing. Reproduction. of 1921 ed.

Bonaparte, Napoleon. <http://www.goodreads.com/quotes/show/255548>. Accessed January 12, 2012.

BrainyQuote.com. Xplore Inc, 2012. <http://www.brainyquote.com/quotes/quotes/n/napoleonbo378985.html>. Accessed January 17, 2012.

Buffet, Warren. *The New York Times.* August 14, 2011. <http://www.nytimes.com/2011/08/15/opinion/stop-coddling-the-super-rich.html>. Accessed March 12, 2012.

Byrne, Alice Hill. *Titus Pomponius Atticus: Chapters of a Biography. A Dissertation*

Presented to the Faculty of Bryn Mawr College in Partial Fulfillment of the Requirements for the Degree of Doctor of Philosophy. Bryn Mawr, Pennsylvania, 1919. Charleston: Bibliolife, LLC.

Byrne, John A. with Gerdes, Lindsey. "The Man Who Invented Management." *Bloomberg/Businessweek.* November 28, 2005. Accessed March 4, 2012. <http://www.businessweek.com/magazine/content/05_48/b3961001.htm>.

Chernow, Ron *The House of Morgan: An American Banking Dynasty and the Rise of Modern Finance.* New York: Grove Press, 2010.

Conrad, Edward. *Unintended Consequences.* New York: Portfolio/Penguin, 2012.

Churchill, Winston. Speech, House of Commons, May 2, 1935. <http://www.quotationspage.com/quote/41363.html>. Accessed January 16, 2012.

Disraeli, Benjamin. *Endymion: General Historical Collections.* British Library, Historical Print Editions, 1880.

Drucker, Peter F. *Managing in Turbulent Times.* New York: HarperCollins, 2006.

Drummond, A. "The Dictator Years." *Historia: Zeitschrift für Alte Geschichte.* Bd. 27, H. 4 (4th Qtr., 1978), pp. 550-572. Published by: Franz Steiner Verlag.

Appendix F - Bibliography

Everitt, Anthony. *The Life and Times of Rome's Greatest Politician, Cicero.* New York: Random House, 2003.

Everitt, Anthony. *Augustus: The Life of Rome's First Emperor.* New York: Random House, 2006.

Finley, M. I. *The Ancient Economy.* (Foreword by Morris, I.) Berkeley: California University Press, 1999.

Flower, Harriet I. *Roman Republics.* (Kindle Edition). Princeton University Press, 2011.

Franklin, Benjamin. <http://en.wikiquote.org/wiki/Ben_Franklin>. Accessed March 16, 2012.

BrainyQuote.com. Xplore Inc. <http://www.brainyquote.com/quotes/quotes/b/benjaminfr132478.html>. Accessed January 17, 2012.

Goodman, Rob and Soni, Jimmy. *Rome's Last Citizen: The Life and Legacy of Cato, Mortal Enemy of Caesar.* New York: Thomas Dunne Books, 2012.

Grant, Michael. *The Ancient Historians.* New York: Barnes and Noble, Inc, 1970.

Gruen, Erich S. *The Last Generation of the Roman Republic.* Berkeley: University of California Press, 1995.

Hill, H. *The Roman Middle Class in the Republican Period.* Westport: Greenwood Press, 1974..

Holland, Tom. *Rubicon: The Last Years of the Republic*. New York: Anchor Books, 2003.

Horsfall, Nicholas. "Prose and Mime." *Latin Literature*. Eds. E. J. Kenney and W. V. Clausen. Cambridge University Press, 1982. *Cambridge Histories Online*. Cambridge University Press. 26 January 2012. DOI:10.1017/ CHOL9780521210430.015: 290-293.

Jones, David. *The Bankers Of Puteoli: Finance, Trade and Industry in the Roman World*. Gloucestershire: Tempus Publishing Limited, 2006.

Kramp Geweke, Lenore. "Notes on the Political Relationship of Cicero and Atticus from 56 to 43 B.C." *The Classical Journal*. Vol. 32, No. 8 (May, 1937), pp. 467-481. The Classical Association of the Middle West and South. <http://www.jstor.org/stable/3291068>. Accessed December 16, 2011.

Meier, Christian. *Caesar*. London: Harper Collins Publishers, 1982.

Mencken, H.L. <http://en.wikiquote.org/wiki/Politics>. Accessed March 16, 2012.

Miles, Margret, M. *Art as Plunder: The Origins of Debate about Cultural Property*. Cambridge: Cambridge University Press, 2008.

Millar, Fergus. *Rome, the Greek World and the East*. Vol.I: The Roman Republic and the

Appendix F - Bibliography

Augustan Revolution. Chapel Hill: The University of North Carolina Press, 2002.

Millar, Fergus. *The Crowd in Rome in the Late Republic*. Ann Arbor: The University of Michigan Press, 1998.

Nicholson, John. "The Delivery and Confidentiality of Cicero's Letters." *The Classical Journal*. Vol. 90, No. 1 (Oct.- Nov., 1994), pp. 33-63.

Oldfather, W. A. "A Nuance in the Friendship of Cicero and Atticus." *The Classical Journal*. Vol. 26, No. 2 (Nov., 1930), pp. 143-144. The Classical Association of the Middle West and South.

Orwell, George. *The Orwell Reader*. San Diego: Harcourt, 1984.

Osgood, Josiah. *Caesar's Legacy: Civil War and the Emergence of the Roman Empire*. New York: Cambridge University Press, 2006.

Phillips, John J. "Atticus and the Publication of Cicero's Works." *The Classical World*. Vol. 79, No. 4 (Mar. - Apr., 1986), pp. 227-237. Classical Association of the Atlantic States.

Pulp Fiction (1994). <http://www.pulpfiction.com/news-mr-wolfs-first-scene.html>. Accessed January 16, 2012.

Raaflaub, Kurt A., Toher, Mark. (ed.) *Between Republic and Empire: Interpretations of Augustus and His Principate*.

Berkeley: University of California Press, 1993.

Rawson, Elizabeth. *Cicero: A Portrait*. London: Bristol Classical Paperbacks, 2009.

RealtyTrac. "Record 2.9 Million U.S. Properties Receive Foreclosure Filings in 2010 Despite 30-Month Low in December". (January 12, 2011). <http://www.realtytrac.com/content/press-releases/record-2.9-million-us-properties-receive-foreclosure-filings-in-2010-despite-30-month-low-in-december-6309>. Accessed January 23, 2012.

Richard, Carl J. *The Founders and the Classics: Greece, Rome and the American Enlightenment*. Cambridge: Harvard University Press, 1994.

Roosevelt, Theodore. <http://www.iperceptive.com/authors/theodore_roosevelt_quotes.html>. (Quoted in *The Works of Theodore Roosevelt*, 1926). Accessed March 15, 2012.

Sampson, Gareth, C. *The Defeat of Rome in the East: Crassus, The Parthians, and the Disastrous Battle of Carrhae, 53BC*. Drexel Hill: Casemate, 2008.

Sear, David R. *Roman Coins and Their Values*. London: Spink and Son Ltd., 2000.

Shakespeare, William. *Julius Caesar*. Stillwell: Digireads.com Publishing, 2005.

Appendix F - Bibliography

Shiff, Stacy. *Cleopatra: A Life*. New York: Back Bay Books, 2010.

Southern, Pat. *Augustus*. New York: Routledge, 2001.

Strauss, Barry. *The Spartacus War*. New York: Simon and Schuster, 2009.

Syme, Ronald. *The Roman Revolution*. New York: Oxford University Press, 1960.

Tempest, Kathryn. *Cicero: Politics and Persuasion in Ancient Rome*. London: Continuum International Publishing Group, 2001.

The Godfather (1972). A scene between Tom Hagen (Robert Duvall) and Sonny Corleone (James Caan). <http://www.imdb.com/character/ch0000812/quotes>. Accessed January 16, 2012.

The New American Bible. Wichita: Fireside Bible Publishers, 1981.

Titchener, Frances. "Cornelius Nepos and the Biographical Tradition." *Greece & Rome*. Second Series, Vol. 50, No. 1 (Apr., 2003), pp. 85-99. Cambridge University Press on behalf of The Classical Association.

Trump, Donald. <http://www.successories.com/iquote/author/1298/donald-trump-quotes/1>. Accessed January 15, 2012.

United States Courts. *Bankruptcy Statistics*. Accessed January 23, 2012. <http://www.uscourts.gov/Statistics/BankruptcyStatistics.aspx>.

Welch, Kathryn E. "T. Pomponius Atticus: A Banker in Politics?" *Historia: Zeitschrift für Alte Geschichte*. Bd. 45, H. 4 (4th Qtr., 1996), pp. 450-471.

Wootton, David, (Trans.). *Machiavelli: The Prince*. Indianapolis; Hacket Publishing Company Inc., 1995.

Index of Names

A

Agrippa. *See Marcus Vipsanius Agrippa.*

Antonius. *See Mark Antony.*

Antony. *See Mark Antony.*

Atticus 31-34.

    and Antony 20-21, 134-136, 139, 147-149, 152-153.

    and art 18, 85-86, 105, 120, 122, 173.

    and Brutus 125-126, 129-130, 132-136, 138, 140, 149.

    and Caesar 106-108, 111, 113, 158-159, 161-164.

    and Cicero 24, 44, 58-59, 71, 76, 80-83, 85-88, 95, 97-101, 103-104, 107-108, 111, 114-115, 140-141, 159, 163, 179-180.

    and Cleopatra 113-114.

    and his assets 47, 51-52, 57, 94-95, 179.

and his father 40-42, 44, 46.
and his literary efforts 24-25, 157-159.
and his maternal uncle, Caecilius 94-95.
and Nepos 24-25, 41-42, 158, 171, 179.
and his politics 98-100, 163.
and his position in society 22-23.
and his uncle, Sulpicius 39, 46-47, 49.
and his withdrawal from Rome 48-49, 51, 53.
and modern historians 21-22.
and Octavian 152-153.
and Pompey 103, 105-108, 111, 120-122.
and Sicyon 85-88.
and Sulla 39, 47, 53, 72-74.
as a role model 20-21.
and the Athenians 48, 54-55, 60-62.
and the Optimates 98-99, 101, 105, 107, 126, 133.
death of 165-166.
Lesson 1: on self-promotion 43, 63, 167.
Lesson 2: on cultivating the powerful 45, 63, 167.
Lesson 3: on getting out of Dodge 49-50, 64, 137, 167.
Lesson 4: on cash management 52, 64, 167.
Lesson 5: on firmness of purpose 56, 64, 167.
Lesson 6: on the value of overstatement 59, 64, 168.
Lesson 7: on time management 61-62, 65, 168.

Index of Names

Lesson 8: on neutrality 74-75, 90, 168.

Lesson 9: on who you know 78-79, 90, 168.

Lesson 10: on self-preservation 83, 90, 168.

Lesson 11: on tenacity 86-87, 90, 168.

Lesson 12: on the virtue of skepticism 96, 116, 168.

Lesson 13: on controlling passion 101-102, 116, 168.

Lesson 14: on decision-making 108-109, 117, 168.

Lesson 15: on adaptation 112, 117, 168.

Lesson 16: on listening 126-127, 143, 168.

Lesson 17: on not persisting in error 130, 143, 168.

Lesson 18: on hedging your bets 137, 143, 168.

Lesson 19: on politics as a marathon 149, 156, 168.

Lesson 20: on justifying the means 153-154, 156, 168.

lifestyle of 97, 179-180.

literary efforts of 157-159, 161-164.

stakeholders of 89, 115, 142, 156

B

Bonaparte, Napoleon 56-57, 87-88.

Brutus. *See Marcus Brutus.*

Buffet, Warren 45.

Byrne, Alice Hill 161.

C

Camuccini, Vincenzo 122.

Caesar. *See Julius Caesar.*

Caesar Augustus. *See Octavian.*

Churchill, Winston 108-110.

Cicero. *See Marcus Tullius Cicero.*

Caecilius. *See Quintus Caecilius.*

Cassius. *See Gaius Cassius.*

Christ. *See Jesus.*

Cleopatra 113-114.

Corleone, Sonny 84.

Cornelius Nepos 29, 31, 33, 35.
    and Cicero, 173-175.
    and his book dedication to Atticus 166-167.
    and the Optimates 125.
    as a biographer of Atticus 24-25, 171-172.
    on Atticus and Brutus 129, 161-162.
    on Atticus and Caesar 110, 125.
    on Atticus and Cicero 44, 80-83, 85-86.
    on Atticus and Mark Antony 132, 134, 146-147, 149.
    on Atticus and Optimates 98-99.
    on Atticus and Pompey 103, 105.
    on Atticus and Sulla 72-74.
    on Atticus and the Athenians 48, 54-55, 58-61.
    on Atticus and triumvirs 152, 153.

Index of Names

    on Atticus the author 157-159.

    on the personal life of Atticus 40-42, 44-47, 76-78, 97-98, 179-180.

Crassus. *See Marcus Crassus.*

D

Dante 75.

David, Jacques-Louise, 26,57.

Darwin, Charles 112.

Decimus Brutus 125.

Dio Cassius 120.

Disraeli, Benjamin 137.

Drucker, Peter 18.

E

Everitt, Antony 27.

F

Franklin, Benjamin 101-102.

Fulvia 134-135, 148-149.

Furius 177.

G

Gaius Cassius 32-33, 119-120, 124-125, 131-132, 138, 141, 145, 147, 150.

Gaius Julius Caesar Augustus. *See Octavian.*
Gaius Marius 31, 33, 35, 39-40, 44, 46-47, 70, 89.
Gaius Octavius. *See Octavian.*
Galbraith, John Kenneth, 43-44.
Gérôme, Jean-Leon 123.
Gaius Verres 173-175.

H

Herennius 148.
Hitler, Adolph 109.
Horsfall, Nicholas 172, 175.
Houdon, Jean-Antoine, 102.

J

Jesus 74.
Johnson, Lyndon Baines, 43.
Julia 31, 33, 91-92.
Julius Caesar 10, 19-21, 23, 31-35, 41, 72, 81, 89, 103, 105, 133, 136, 139-140, 142-143, 145-146, 152, 155.
    and Atticus 106-108, 111, 113, 158-159.
    and Brutus 151, 162-164.
    and Cicero 100-101, 110, 114-115, 160.
    and Sulla 70-71.
    and the first triumvirate 31, 91-92, 177.

Index of Names

assassination 119-126, 128-130, 138.

crossing the Rubicon 93.

funeral of 131-132.

Julius Caesar Octavianus. *See Octavian.*

K

Kennedy, John F. 43, 75.

L

Laelius 177.

Lepidus 32-34, 145-146, 152.

Lucius Cornelius Sulla 31, 33-35, 39, 46-47, 53, 55, 69-72, 85, 89, 92-93, 94, 99, 147.

and Caesar 70, 72.

and Cicero 71, 72.

and Crassus 68-69, 72.

and Atticus 72-74.

and political factions 28, 36-38.

and Pompey 68-69, 72.

rise of 38.

treatment of enemies 67-68.

Lucius Junius Brutus 25-26, 162-163.

Lucius Plaetorius Cestianus 151.

Lucius Torquatus 44, 85.

L. Lucullus 94-95.

M

Maccari, Cesare, 131.

Machiavelli, Niccolo 153-155.

Marcus Brutus 19, 21, 23, 32-33, 89, 115, 119, 141-142, 145, 147, 156, 159-160.
- and Atticus 125-126, 129-130, 132-136, 138, 140, 149.
- and Atticus' genealogy 161-164.
- and Caesar's assassination 120-123, 128.
- and Caesar's will 124.
- and control of government 125, 131-132.
- and intimacy with Atticus 126, 129.
- defeat of 150.
- link to Caesar 163.
- reputation of 151.

Marcus Crassus 31, 33-34, 68-69, 72, 81, 89, 91-92, 115, 146, 177.

Marcus Tullius Cicero 19, 21, 23-25, 27, 29-33, 35, 44, 67, 72, 76, 89, 131, 138, 142, 145, 156.
- and Antony 21, 123, 128, 130, 133-136, 139-141, 146-148.
- and Caesar's assassination 122-123, 125-126.
- and Cleopatra 113.
- and his constraints 100-101, 114-115.
- and Nepos 173-175.
- and Octavian 140-141, 146, 146-147.

Index of Names

 and self-censorship 177.

 as a Caesarian apologist 160.

 at the wedding of Atticus 97.

 consul 85, 141.

 death of 146-148, 155.

 exile of 76, 80-83, 92, 98.

 friendship with Atticus 24, 44, 71, 81.

 on books of Atticus 159.

 on the Caecilius affair 95.

 on the generosity of Atticus 58-59.

 on the politics of Atticus 98-100, 163.

 on personal life of Atticus 97, 179-180.

 on Sicyon 85-88.

 politics of 99-101, 103-104, 107-108, 111, 114-115, 140-141, 146-148, 152.

 rising star 71-72.

Marcus Vipsanius Agrippa 32-33, 145, 165.

 and death of Atticus 165.

 and the Pantheon 153.

 marriage to Atticus' daughter 152-153.

Marius. *See Gaius Marius.*

Mark Antony 19-21, 23, 32-34, 89, 115, 119, 142, 145, 156, 164, 174-175.

 and Atticus 20-21, 134-136, 139, 147-149, 152-153.

 and Caesar's death 124, 128, 130-132.

and Cicero's execution 148-149.
and Cicero's knowledge of Caesar's murder 123-124.
and Octavian 146-147, 150, 152-153, 155, 165.
succeeds Caesar 132, 134-136, 139-141.

Maximus. *See Valerius Maximus.*
Mencken, H. L. 127.
Miles, Margaret M. 172-175.
Morgan, J. Pierpont 96.

N

Nepos. *See Cornelius Nepos.*
Northen, Adolf 88.

O

Octavian 32-34, 115, 124-125, 133-134, 139-142, 145-147, 150-153, 155-156, 164-165.
Oppius 100.
Orwell, George 149-150.

P

Pilia 31-32, 34, 91, 97, 119, 142.
von Piloty, Karl Theodor 121.
Pliny the Elder 86.
Plutarch 67, 120-123, 126, 148, 162-163.

Pompey 31, 33-34, 68-69, 72, 81, 89, 91-93, 100, 110, 114-115, 123, 146, 177.
and Atticus 103, 105-108, 111, 120-122.
Pompey the Great. *See Pompey.*
Pontius Pilate 164.

Q

Quintus Caecilius 31, 33, 91, 94-95.
Quintus Tullius Cicero 81-82, 110-111.

R

Roosevelt, Theodore 62.

S

Santi di Tito, 154.
Servilia 163.
Shackleton Bailey, D. R. 21, 104.
Shakespeare 21, 23, 70, 163.
Suetonius 146, 163.
Sulla. *See Lucius Cornelius Sulla.*
Sulpicius 39, 46-47, 49.
Sylla. *See Lucius Cornelius Sulla.*

T

Tiberius 165-166.

Titchener, Frances 172.

Travolta, John 50.

Trump, Donald 59-60.

V

Valerius Maximus 94-95.

Verres. *See Gaius Verres.*

W

Welch, Kathryn E. 53, 81, 158.

Y

Young Caesar. *See Octavian.*

Younger Gaius Marius 44.

About the Author

Bob is a retired business executive whose career spanned more than 30 years in the high tech industry. Bob began his professional career at Xerox Corporation after he obtained a Bachelor of Science degree in Physics from Worcester Polytechnic Institute and an MBA from the University of Rochester's Simon School of Business.
In 1980 Bob joined Wang Laboratories and spent twenty years with Wang and its successor companies in a variety of product development, marketing, sales and service management positions. Following Wang's emergence from bankruptcy in 1993 as Wang Global, Bob was named President of Wang Canada and following his turnaround of that operation, Bob was appointed President of Wang Global's North American Field Service operation with responsibility

for over 4,000 employees and revenues of more than half a billion dollars.

In 2000, following Getronics NV's acquisition of Wang Global, Bob led a management buyout of a division of Getronics and was appointed President and CEO of QualxServ, the newly formed company. Under Bob's leadership QualxServ grew into a global computer services provider spanning more than a dozen countries and employing over 3,000 computer service professionals worldwide.

After spending nearly a decade with QualxServ, Bob retired from his position as President and CEO in 2009 and stepped down from QualxServ's Board in 2010 (the company has since been renamed Worldwide TechServices). Retirement has allowed Bob to spend more time with his wife Diane and daughters Meredith and Allison as well as pursue his passion for the study of the business management lessons that can be learned from ancient Rome.

Bob remains a consultant to Worldwide TechServices, serves as an Advisor to Work Market, a web-based labor management company and is a member of both the Simon School of Business Advisory Council and the George Eastman Circle at the University of Rochester.

LESSONS FROM
HISTORY

About the Series

This series is for primarily business and IT professionals looking for inspiration for their projects. Specifically, business managers responsible for solving business problems, or Project Managers (PMs) responsible for delivering business solutions through IT projects.

This series uses relevant historical case studies to examine how historical projects and emerging technologies of the past solved complex problems. It then draws comparisons to challenges encountered in today's IT projects.

This series benefits the reader in several ways:

- It outlines the stages involved in delivering a complex IT project providing a step-by-step guide to the project deliverables.

- It vividly describes the crucial lessons from historical projects and complements these with some of today's best practices.

- It makes the whole learning experience more memorable.

The series should inspire the reader as these historical projects were achieved with a lesser (inferior) technology.

Website: http://www.lessons-from-history.com/

Did you like this book?

If you enjoyed this book, you will find more interesting books at

www.MMPubs.com

Please take the time to let us know how you liked this book. Even short reviews of 2-3 sentences can be helpful and may be used in our marketing materials. If you take the time to post a review for this book on Amazon.com, let us know when the review is posted and you will receive a free audiobook or ebook from our catalog. Simply email the link to the review once it is live on Amazon.com, with your name and your mailing address—send the email to orders@mmpubs.com with the subject line "Book Review Posted on Amazon."

If you have questions about this book, our customer loyalty program, or our review rewards program, please contact us at info@mmpubs.com.

Oshawa, Ontario, Canada

Entrepreneurship and Ethics in Ancient Rome: The Management Lessons of Pliny the Younger

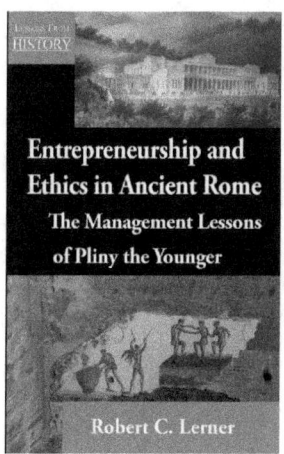

It was fall and the late summer rains had produced an overly-abundant grape harvest. Such a large harvest was driving down grape prices. Brokers who bought grape futures at premium prices early in the summer would be selling at a tremendous loss. The largest growers faced a dilemma: hold brokers to their contracts, causing longer-term disruption in the futures market; or renegotiate supply contracts to ease the financial burden on the brokers, ensuring a stable marketplace and building customer loyalty.

What may surprise you is that this challenging scenario ocurred 1,900 years ago during the Roman Empire. Many of our modern business problems were confronted then – and resolved – without the aid of modern technologies.

This book reveals how one ancient entrepreneur overcame this challenge to maintain customer loyalty, manage his sales channel, motivate people, resolve conflicts and ethical dilemmas, and more. The book reveals lessons learned that can be applied to today's business environment.

ISBN-13:   9781554891313   (paperback)

Available in print and electronic formats. Order directly from the publisher at **www.mmpubs.com**.

Project Lessons from the Roman Empire: An Ancient Guide to Modern Project Management

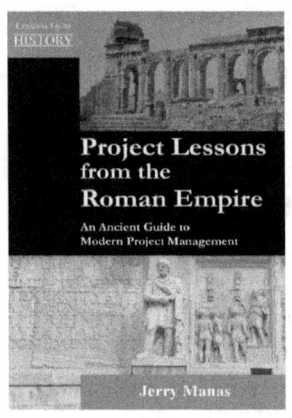

The leaders of the Roman Empire established many of the organizational governance practices that we follow today, in addition to remarkable feats of engineering using primitive tools that produced roads and bridges which are still being used today, complex irrigation systems, and even "flush toilets." Yet, the leaders were challenged with political intrigue, rebelling team members, and pressure from the competition. How could they achieve such long-lasting greatness in the face of these challenges?

In this new addition to the Lessons from History series, join author Jerry Manas as he takes you on a journey through history to learn about project management the Roman way. Discover the 23 key lessons that can be learned from the successes and failures of the Roman leadership, with specific advice on how they can be applied to today's projects.

Read this intriguing book to learn how they did it.

ISBN-13:   9781554890545   (paperback)

Available in print and electronic formats. Order directly from the publisher at **www.mmpubs.com**.

The History of Project Management

The Pyramid of Giza, the Colosseum, and the Transcontinental Railroad are all great historical projects from the past four millennia. When we look back, we tend to look at these as great architectural or engineering works. Project management tends to be overlooked, and yet its core principles were used extensively in these projects.

Mark Kozak-Holland explores the history of project management and how it evolved over the past 4,500 years. This book shows that "modern" project management practices did not just appear in the past 100 years but have been used — often with a lot of sophistication — for thousands of years.

As readers explore the many case studies in this book, they will discover fascinating details of innovative projects that produced many of our most famous landmarks and voyages of discovery.

ISBN-13:   9781554890965   (Hardcover)

Available in print and electronic formats. Order directly from the publisher at **www.mmpubs.com**.

Project Management Blunders: Lessons from the Project that Built, Launched, and Sank Titanic

White Star's initiative to build its new Olympic-class ships can be described as a text book project. It started off very well in the initiation and planning phases: the project team had a very good understanding of the business and customer needs, a solid vision, a superlative business case, the right supplier partnerships, good stakeholder relationships, and a healthy balance of proven and emerging technologies.

By the end of the design phase, however, decisions were made that compromised safety features. By the end of the fitting-out phase, all key stakeholders believed that the ships could never founder.

Mark Kozak-Holland reveals the project management blunders that doomed *Titanic* while it was still being built. Filled with photos and copies of actual documents from the project, this book walks you through a case study in project management failure.

ISBN-13:   9781554891221   (paperback)

Available in print and electronic formats. Order directly from the publisher at **www.mmpubs.com**.

Titanic Lessons in Project Leadership: Effective Communication and Team Building

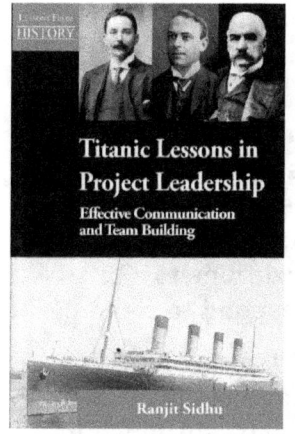

In *Titanic Lessons in Project Leadership* we see how "small" and easily overlooked behavioral and communication issues can aggregate through a project to become seemingly unthinkable errors.

This book focuses on the people aspects of the *Titanic* story; the key stakeholders, power dynamics, underlying perceptions, communication, leadership and team interactions. Ranjit Sidhu draws on this tragic tale to focus on the "behind the scenes" aspects of human communication and leadership to guide you in the right direction for making that vital difference to your current projects.

Combining contemporary management theory with her own insights and extensive project management experience, Ranjit offers practical guidance and lessons from history that will help you gain a deeper understanding of how leaders and teams can operate at their very best.

ISBN-13:   9781554891207   (paperback)

Available in print and electronic formats. Order directly from the publisher at **www.mmpubs.com**.

Polaris: Lessons in Risk Management

Risk management is one of the most important practices that a manager can employ to help drive a successful outcome from a project. Good risk management allows organizations to proactively respond to risks.

Unfortunately, many managers believe risk management to be too time consuming or too complicated. Some find it to be shrouded in mystery.

This book by Dr. John J. Byrne, PMP is designed to demystify risk management, explaining introductory and advanced risk management approaches in simple language. This book uses real-life examples from a very influential project that helped change the course of world history -- the project that designed and built the *Polaris* missile and accompanying submarine launch system that became a key deterrent to a Soviet nuclear attack during the Cold War.

Containing a foreword by James R. Snyder, one of the founders of the Project Management Institute (PMI), this book is structured to align with the risk management approach described in PMI's the *Project Management Body of Knowledge (PMBOK Guide)*.

ISBN-13:   9781554890972 (Paperback)

Available in print and electronic formats. Order directly from the publisher at **www.mmpubs.com**.

Agile Leadership and the Management of Change: Project Lessons from Winston Churchill and the Battle of Britain

Around the turn of the millennium, there was a poll conducted in Britain that asked who people thought was the most influential person in all of Britain's history. The winner: Winston Churchill. What set Churchill above the others was his leadership qualities: his ability to create and share a powerful vision, his ability to motivate the population in the face of tremendous fear, and his ability to get others to rally behind him and quickly turn his visions into reality. By any measure, Winston Churchill was a powerful leader.

What many don't know, however, was how Churchill used his leadership skills to restructure the British military, government, and even the British manufacturing sector to support his efforts to rearm the country and get ready for an imminent enemy invasion in early 1940.

Join author Mark Kozak-Holland as he explores how Churchill acted as the head project manager of a massive change project that affected the daily lives of millions of people. Learn about Churchill's change management and agile management techniques and how they can be applied to today's projects.

ISBN-13:   9781554890354   (Paperback)

Available in print and electronic formats. Order directly from the publisher at **www.mmpubs.com**.

www.ingramcontent.com/pod-product-compliance
Lightning Source LLC
Chambersburg PA
CBHW070337240426
43665CB00045B/2147